Anonymous

Indianapolis Cook Book

Anonymous

Indianapolis Cook Book

ISBN/EAN: 9783744781305

Printed in Europe, USA, Canada, Australia, Japan

Cover: Foto ©Lupo / pixelio.de

More available books at **www.hansebooks.com**

INDIANAPOLIS

COOK BOOK,

COMPILED BY

THE LADIES

OF THE

PATTISON METHODIST EPISCOPAL CHURCH,

INDIANAPOLIS, IND.

She looketh well to the ways of her household, and eateth not the bread of idleness.

Give her of the fruit of her hands, and let her own works praise her in the gates.—PROVERBS XXXI, 27 and 31.

INDIANAPOLIS:
HASSELMAN—JOURNAL CO. PRINT.
1883.

PREFACE.

The ladies of the Pattison M. E. church, desiring to assist in the work of re-building the church, decided to publish a cook book, hoping that it would be acceptable to the public and meet with a large sale.

During the preparation and arrangement of recipes and directions, the committee has received much encouragement. The contribution of valuable recipes from other Indianapolis ladies, and from friends at a distance, have been gratefully received and appreciated.

The advertisements of leading business firms will very materially assist in defraying expense of publication.

With so much inspiration received, and so much effort already expended, those most interested in the cause will prosecute it with vigor. The book, it is believed, will not disappoint the purchaser.

The recipes are good and practical; adapted to the wants of the most fastidious; of those who desire elaborate cooking or who wish to prepare for large companies, and of those who have a limited purse, plain taste, and upon whom society makes few demands.

It will be noticed that "The Indianapolis Cook Book" is a temperance book. Not a drop of that which intoxicates is recommended in any recipe for fruit cake, pudding-sauce or mince pie—and not even in the excellent medical department.

Indianapolis, Ind., December 20th, 1882.

INDIANAPOLIS COOK BOOK.

BUTTER, BREAD, Etc.

BUTTER.
Mrs. Owings, Sr.

Have crocks very clean. Don't put them on the stove, nor in the oven, but scald them with hot water. Never put warm milk, such as strippings, in your sour-milk or cream jar. Don't let the milk stand longer than to get thick. If it keeps sweet, it is well to put buttermilk in it the night before churning, so that it will be ready to churn. The milk from different cows differs in the length of time for bringing the butter. Some will form the butter in five minutes, some in fifteen, and some in an hour. It is best to churn slowly until the milk is the right temperature. If it needs to be warmer, warm water can be added; if cooler, cold water. Wash the buttermilk all out with water, and add salt as you work it.

BUTTER.
Mrs. Black.

If in winter, set the crock of sour cream in a vessel of hot water, and stir until the heat is even. Scald the churn with well water. Bring the milk or cream to a temperature of 72° F. When the butter breaks, empty a bucket of cold water into the churn. Let it stand a few minutes until the granules of butter are hardened. Draw off the buttermilk, and strain it through a sieve. Put more water with the butter in the churn, having dissolved salt in the water. Rinse the butter two or three times, and draw off the water. Great care needs to be taken of the churn after churning to keep it sweet. Good soapsuds should stand in it, and be dashed about; then hot water to take away all the soap; then cold well water.

BUTTER.
Mrs. Robertson, Sr.

After churning until the butter breaks, gather it by dashing a little cold water around the churn; but never wash the buttermilk out with water, unless the butter is to be used immediately. To keep it, and especially to pack it, the buttermilk should be beaten out with paddle, or absorbed by the salt.

BREAD.
Mrs. Black.

The health of the family is very dependent upon good bread. Good flour, good yeast, and great care are necessary. It is important to sift the flour. Good flour will easily crumble after being pressed in the hand. Yeast may be tried by adding a little to a small quantity of flour, and putting it in a warm place. If it rises, or lightens in ten minutes, it is right to use. It is well to make the sponge at night, in winter, and the dough next morning in time to be baked by ten o'clock. In the summer, it may be all made and baked in one day. The sponge may be baked in muffin rings, or on a griddle, for breakfast; or if very thick, can be touched lightly, in shaping rolls, that will very soon rise. Good bread dough can be made into cake, rusk, dumplings, chicken, or fruit pie. It should not stand very long in baking pans. If light when molded, it may sour or lose its freshness, and the sooner become dry and tasteless.

STOCK YEAST.
Mrs. T. H. K. Enos.

Grate six large potatoes, raw. Boil a handful of hops, ten minutes. Strain this hop water upon the grated potatoes, and boil slowly until thoroughly cooked. Add a half teacup of salt and one of sugar. After it has cooled, put in one cup of good yeast, and let it rise. Then bottle, or put it in a jar with tight-fitting cover. In making bread, use one cup of this yeast for potato sponge. The grated potato can be kept white by being put into the hop-water as fast as grated.

SELF-WORKING YEAST.
Marion Harland.

Eight potatoes, two ounces hops, four quarts cold water, one pound of flour, one-half pound white sugar, one tablespoonful salt. Tie the hops in a coarse muslin bag and boil one hour in four quarts of water. Wet the flour with the hop water. Put in the sugar and salt, and beat up the batter. Set it away for two days in an open bowl covered with a thin cloth, where it is moderately and evenly warm. On the third day, peel, boil and mash the potatoes, and stir in the thin batter. After it has stood twelve hours in the warm kitchen, put it away in perfectly clean and sweet jars. This yeast will keep four weeks in a cold cellar.

POTATO YEAST.
Mrs. Benson.

Take four potatoes and boil. Pour the potato water over one pint of flour. Then mash the potatoes; or better, put them through the cullander that there may be no lumps; and when cool, add a cup of good yeast.

DRY YEAST.
Mrs. Ferrell.

Thicken your stock yeast with corn meal, roll out, and cut in cakes. Dry them in the air, turning them often. Make enough in May to last all summer; and in October, for winter use.

BREAD.
Mrs. Hereth.

Make potato yeast in the evening, and early next morning make bread sponge. For six loaves of bread, make a thick batter of flour and two quarts of water. Add the potato yeast, and afterwards one tablespoonful of salt, one of sugar, and one of lard. Set to rise, and when risen, knead it well, and if it rises again before being made into loaves, it will be the whiter and better.

POTATO YEAST.
Mrs. Patton.

Boil and mash six potatoes; pour boiling water on them, in which a bag of hops has been boiled; thicken with sifted flour, and when cooled, add one small cake of compressed yeast, or any other good yeast.

BREAD.
Miss Bugbee.

Two quarts of flour, one large tablespoonful of salt, a teacup of yeast, one pint of warm milk, and one tablespoonful of sugar. Mix stiff with flour and let it rise. Then knead, and put into pans.

SOUR-MILK BREAD.
Mrs. Kring.

Scald one quart of sour milk. When cool enough, set your sponge with the whey. Take one quart of flour, one tablespoon of salt, one teacup of yeast, and stir stiff with a spoon. In the morning, add flour and knead well. Set in pans to rise.

MILK BREAD.

One quart milk, one teacup yeast, one-half teacup butter, and one tablespoon white sugar. Let the milk be warm, add to it the flour and sugar. Beat all together and let them rise four hours. Add melted butter, and lastly, the yeast and salt. In warm weather it will probably be necessary to add a teaspoonful of soda dissolved in warm water, as the milk may sour.

BREAD WITH DRY YEAST.
Miss Sue Bugbee.
In the evening, make a potato sponge with four potatoes boiled and mashed in a cup of flour. When cool, add a cake of yeast that has been soaked in tepid water. Next morning, add one quart of milk, two tablespoonsful salt and flour to make a dough. Knead well, and let it rise and make into loaves. When they are light, bake one hour.

ACTON BREAD.
Mrs. Ella Miller.
Put thin slices of stale bread in milk with beaten egg, and a little sugar. When soaked, fry in hot lard.

SWEET BREAD.
Mrs. Ella Miller.
One cup yeast, one cup milk, one cup sugar, one cup currants or chopped raisins, one-half cup butter; stir in flour and let rise. When light make into a loaf. Spread with butter and sugar before baking.

RYE BREAD.
Mrs. Enos.
Make a sponge of one quart water, one teacup yeast and rye flour; let it rise in a warm place; scald one pint of corn meal; when cool add it to the sponge and knead with rye flour; put into deep pans. Wheat flour may be used instead of the rye.

HOMINY BREAD.
Mrs. Van Wagenen.
Take about two teacups of fine hominy or grits, and while hot mix with it a large spoonful of butter; beat four eggs very light and stir them into the hominy; next add a pint of milk, gradually stirred in; and lastly, half a pint of corn meal. The batter should be of the consistency of a rich, boiled custard; if thicker add a little more milk. Bake with a good deal of heat at the bottom of the oven

and not too much at the top, so as to allow it to rise. The pan in which it is baked ought to be a deep one, to allow space for rising. It has the appearance, when cooked, of a batter pudding, and when rich and well cooked it has almost the delicacy of a baked custard. Cut with a pie knife. Bake about an hour.

RICE BREAD.
Mrs. Black.

Make a sponge of warm water, one cup yeast, one spoon sugar, two spoons lard and one quart wheat flour; beat well, and in five hours add three pints warm milk and three teacups rice flour; wet to a thin paste with cold milk and boil four minutes, as you would boil starch; let it be lukewarm when put into the batter; if not thick enough add wheat flour; knead and put to rise as with wheat bread. If you can not get rice flour boil one cup of whole rice, mash and beat it smooth.

SALT-RISING BREAD.
Mrs. S. E. Wagoner.

In the evening scald one-half cup corn meal; next morning add one pint of warm water, one-half teaspoon salt and a teaspoon of sugar; make a thick batter and keep warm until it rises; mix it soft, knead well, and put into pans immediately. Mashed potatoes improve it.

SALT-RISING BREAD.
Mrs. Sappington.

After breakfast take a cup of new milk and heat quite hot; stir thick with corn meal and keep it warm until next morning; then make a sponge, by taking one quart of milk or warm water, adding salt and one spoonful of sugar, mixing all in the meal. After the sponge has risen mold into loaves and put in pans to rise before baking.

HOMINY BREAD.
Mrs. Sappington.

One cup of hominy grits, boiled soft, three eggs beaten light, one large teaspoon melted lard or butter, about one pint of corn meal, milk enough to make a very thin batter, one tablespoon baking powder, or, if sour milk is used, one teaspoonful of soda.

RICE BREAD.
Mrs. Sappington.

One cup of rice boiled soft, three eggs beaten light, one tablespoon melted lard or butter, one pint corn meal, milk enough to make a very thin batter, one tablespoon baking powder, or, if sour milk is used, one teaspoon soda.

GRAHAM BREAD.
Mrs. Black.

One teacup yeast, one quart warm water, one tablespoon salt, two cups sugar, one small teaspoon soda; add graham flour until stiff enough to drop off the spoon. Grease bread pans and put in the dough. When risen bake in a moderate oven one hour.

BROWN BREAD.
Mrs. Enos.

Use part of the sponge that has been prepared for white bread; add warm water and graham flour; put in one cup of molasses for three loaves of bread. For brown rolls work in a little butter.

BROWN BREAD.
Mrs. Kingsbury.

Three and one-half cups graham flour, two of corn meal, three of sour milk, one-half of molasses, one tablespoon soda; steam two and one-half hours and then put in the oven for fifteen minutes.

GRAHAM BREAD.
Mrs. Hereth.

For one loaf: One quart of flour, two tablespoons molasses, one teaspoon soda, one teaspoon salt, one-half cup yeast; make soft with a spoon; when risen, bake.

QUICK BROWN BREAD.
Mrs. Annie Thurston.

One quart graham flour, one quart corn meal, one teacup molasses, one teaspoon soda, one teaspoon salt and one quart sour milk.

BOSTON BROWN BREAD.
Mrs. Bugbee.

One cup wheat flour, two cups corn meal, one cup rye, one cup molasses, one pint sour milk, one teaspoon soda; steam three hours.

STEAMED BROWN BREAD.
Mrs. Sam Merrill.

Three and one-half cups unbolted flour, one cup corn meal, three teaspoons baking-powder, three-fourths cup molasses, two cups sweet milk, salt; steam two and one-half hours.

YANKEE BROWN BREAD.
Mrs. Hammond.

One quart corn meal, one quart unbolted wheat flour, one teaspoon soda, one pint molasses, one-half pint sour milk, a little salt; put in enough warm water to make a thin batter to pour; steam three hours, bake one hour.

PARKER HOUSE ROLLS.
Mrs. G. M. Pee.

Take two quarts of flour and rub in two tablespoons of lard; boil a pint of sweet milk and let stand until cold; make a hole in the middle of the flour, put in the milk and half a teacup of yeast or half a cake of Fleshman yeast; also two tablespoons sugar and a little salt; let stand until morning, then mix up and let rise three or four times. Instead of kneading down each time pound with a mallet or rolling pin. Roll and cut like pocket-book biscuit.

POCKET-BOOK ROLLS No. 1.
Mrs. Hereth.

Make a potato sponge of six potatoes boiled, and added to flour and water. When cool, add one-half cup potato yeast. When light, add a tablespoon salt, one-half cup lard, and flour for stiff dough. After kneading and setting to rise three times, cut in large biscuit, turning over one-half.

POCKET-BOOK ROLLS No. 2.
Mrs. Springer.

One quart flour, one tablespoon butter, two eggs, one small teacup yeast, one and one-half pints milk. After the batter lightens, make stiff, and when the dough rises, roll thin and spread lightly with butter. Cut with large buscuit cutter, and turn over, like turn-over pies.

STEAMBOAT ROLLS.
Mrs. Ferrell.

On bread-baking day, set aside dough for tea rolls. Work in a tablespoonful of lard. When risen, work again. Cut in rolls one inch thick, five inches long, and one-half inch wide. To make the cleft roll, cut down the center of a roll almost its length, with a sharp knife.

ORDINARY LIGHT ROLLS.
Mrs. Reynolds.

Take bread dough and add lard and a little sugar. Cut either with buscuit cutter or mold with the hand. Put into a well-greased pan and set to rise. When they unite, and then seam, they are ready for the oven.

SUPERIOR ROLLS.
Mrs. Reynolds.

Four cups sweet milk, one small cup lard, add one small cup yeast, and three cups flour. Make this sponge at night. In the morning, add one well-beaten egg. Knead, let rise, and then mold into buscuit.

CINNAMON ROLLS.
Mrs. Herith.

Roll the dough thin, as for pies. Butter, and sprinkle with sugar and cinnamon. Roll this sheet of dough, as for jelly roll. Cut in slices an inch thick. Lay these slices, as you would biscuit, to rise in the pan in which they are to be baked.

PARKER HOUSE ROLLS.
Mrs. Baggs.

Two quarts of flour, one pint of milk, boiled. When cool, add one teaspoon salt, two teaspoons sugar, one teacup yeast. Rub all into the flour. When well risen, work into a loaf and let rise again. Then roll, and cut into cakes; butter each one, fold over and set to rise.

PARKER HOUSE ROLLS No. 2.
Mrs. Baggs.

Make a hole in the center of two quarts of flour. Pour into it one pint of sweet milk that has been boiled, with a small lump of butter in it. Add one-fourth cup sugar, one-fourth cup yeast, and one tablespoon salt. Let it stand two hours or more, and then knead. Set to rise, knead, and mould. Some leave the flour, milk, butter, sugar, yeast, and salt unmixed all night, and next morning beat very hard with a spoon, and immediately stiffen and mould.

IMPERIAL ROLLS.
Mrs. Enos.

Beat one-half cup butter with one tablespoon sugar; roll light dough thin and spread with the butter and sugar; roll a second layer and spread like the first; then a third layer; cut in biscuit size and let stand until light.

ENGLISH ROLLS.

One quart flour, two ounces butter, one-half cup yeast, one pint warm milk; stir well together and set in warm place; when light make into rolls and let rise again.

FRENCH ROLLS No. 1.
Mrs. Spahr, Sr.

One pint milk, one teacup butter, one teacup sugar, three eggs, one teacup yeast, and flour to knead. Let the sponge be made of the milk, yeast and flour. When light add the eggs, butter and sugar, and let rise again.

FRENCH ROLLS No. 2.

Rub one-half teacup of butter into one quart of flour; beat the whites of three eggs well; add one-half cup yeast, a little salt and milk to make stiff dough. Let rise in a warm place, and when risen bake in ten minutes.

EGG ROLLS.
Mrs. Enos.

Two teacups sweet milk, two eggs, a little salt, three and one-half cups flour; bake in hot gem pans.

POP-OVERS.
Miss Crane, Madison, Ind.

One cup milk, one cup flour, one egg, beaten separately; bake in cups, a tablespoon to each cup.

GRAHAM ROLLS.
Mrs. Osborne.

These rolls may be made as ordinary light rolls, only substituting graham for the white flour.

GRAHAM BREAKFAST ROLLS.

Six potatoes boiled and mashed, one pint of water, one-half cup of sugar, one tablespoon salt and one-half cup of yeast; make into a stiff dough with graham flour; let it rise over night; in the morning mold lightly and let rise.

BROWN ROLLS.
Mrs. Black.

One quart graham flour, with milk or water to make batter; one-third cup of yeast; let it rise over night; in the morning add two eggs, one large tablespoon sugar, one-fourth teaspoon soda, a little butter and a little salt; put in cups, gem pans or muffin rings.

GERMAN ROLLS.

Beat thoroughly two eggs; add to them one-half pint milk, one tablespoon butter, one teacup yeast, all poured into the flour and mixed softer than bread; let it rise before baking.

GERMAN COFFEE CAKE.
Mrs. Fletcher Rubush.

Knead and roll out bread sponge, adding lard, one egg and one-half cup sugar; make it three-fourths of an inch thick; crumble together butter, cinnamon and sugar with which to cover the top. It is nice baked in a pie pan.

SALT-RISING BREAD.
Mrs. Rubush.

Set sponge over night in a warm place. Let the sponge be made of flour, water and a little salt. In the morning, add a little fresh, warm batter. After it rises, boil a little sweet milk and scald flour. When cool, stir in the rising, knead well, and put in pans to rise. It can rise in ten or fifteen minutes. A tablespoonful of sugar put in the batter in the morning improves it.

COMPRESSED YEAST BREAD.
Mrs. Rubush.

Make a potato yeast in the morning, by using a small cake of compressed yeast with the mashed potatoes, flour and water. It will be ready to bake before night, if made into dough at noon, kneaded, and set to rise a little while. This yeast lightens quicker than any other.

CORN MEAL YEAST CAKES.
Miss Leslie.

Boil one-half pound of fresh hops in four quarts of water until the liquid is two quarts. Strain it into a pan and mix in flour enough to make a thin batter. Add one-half pint yeast. When fermented, stir in corn meal to make a stiff dough. Cover it, and set in a warm place to rise. When very light, roll out into a sheet an inch thick, and cut into flat cakes four inches square. Spread them out separately to dry in a cool place. While drying, turn them five or six times a day. When hard, put them in brown paper sacks. Dissolve one in a little warm water, thicken with flour; cover, and put near the fire to rise. Then mix with flour for bread, one yeast cake to two quarts of flour.

BUTTERMILK BREAD.
Mrs. Owings, Sr.

Back of the bread is the yeast. Take a large handful of hops; if pressed hops, ten cents worth. Take a large stone jar and fill it two-thirds full of sifted flour. Mix in it one large coffee cup of brown sugar, and one-half cup salt. Boil your hops twenty minutes. Boil eight or ten large potatoes until they are soft, and mash them. Strain the hops and scald the flour with the hops and potato water. Let it be stiff as you can stir it. Add one cup or more of yeast, and as fast as the flour rises, stir it down. In the evening, add the corn meal, by pouring the yeast into a large pan of corn meal. Spread a large, clean table cloth in a warm room, and scatter the crumbled corn meal yeast over it. Use one pint of this yeast, if you want to make six loaves of bread. Scald your flour with buttermilk. When it is cool enough, add the yeast. Set in a warm place to rise. When risen, knead and let rise again. Then put it in pans for last rising. This makes good sweet bread.

SALLY LUNN.
Mrs. Springer.

Six eggs, one quart of milk, five pints of flour and one teacup of yeast. Make a stiff batter and set to rise in pie-pans, after greasing them. Bake when well risen.

SALLY LUNN.
Miss Sanie King, Madison.

One pint warm milk, three eggs, one tablespoon yeast, three spoons lard, one tablespoon sugar, and three pints flour. It will rise and be ready to bake in two or three hours.

SALLY LUNN.
Miss Howell.

Two eggs, three tablespoons sugar, one tablespoon butter, one teacup sweet milk, three teaspoons baking powder in three pints of flour.

SALLY LUNN.
Mrs. Enos.

Three pints flour, two ounces butter melted in one pint warm water, one teaspoon salt, one teacup sugar, three eggs well beaten, one teacup yeast. Beat all together for ten minutes; put in baking-pans; sprinkle sugar on the top after they are baked.

RUSK.
Miss E. McLaughlin.

Make a sponge of one pint milk, one cup sugar, one cup butter, five eggs and one teacup yeast. In the morning make stiff batter and set to rise. When light, make into rolls and set in warm place.

GRANDMA'S RUSK.
Mrs. Graydon.

One quart milk, three-eighths pound butter, three eggs, salt, two tablespoons yeast. Set to rise in one pint milk; melt the butter in the remainder of the milk; add a heaping saucer of white sugar; when the sponge is well raised mix together in a loaf; let it rise well; then make out into rolls and let rise a second time.

RUSK.
Mrs. Levers.

One cup butter, one pint milk, flour to make stiff batter, one cup yeast. When light, add one cup sugar, two eggs, one tablespoon salt, and flour to mould like biscuit. Set to rise.

RUSK.

One pint warm milk, one pint sugar, one cup butter, one cup yeast, one tablespoon salt, and one quart flour. When risen, make into dough, roll out and cut into biscuit.

RUSK.

One pint milk, one-half cup yeast, one and one-half cups white sugar, three eggs, one-half cup butter, one tablespoon cinnamon, and flour for stiff batter. When risen, make into rolls and spread sugar, cinnamon and butter over the top.

RUSK.
Mrs. Levers.

Four cups dough, one-half cup butter, one cup sugar, three eggs, and the flour necessary. After this dough lightens, make into high, narrow rolls, and rub the tops with sugar and water.

WAFERS.

One quart flour, two tablespoons butter, a little salt. Mix with sweet milk; roll as thin as possible; lay in a large biscuit-shape in pan. They are nice rolled up when taken from oven. This is peculiarly Southern.

CRUMPETS.

Make a sponge as for yeast muffins; when light, add melted butter and a little flour; bake in muffin rings.

MUFFINS.

Two eggs, one pint warm milk, one tablespoon melted lard, one-half teacup yeast, salt, flour to make a stiff batter; lighten, and then put batter in gem pans or muffin rings.

MUFFINS.

One-half cup sugar, one-half cup butter two cups milk, an even tablespoon salt, three tablespoons yeast, one quart of flour; when light, or risen, stir in two well-beaten eggs and bake in pans or rings in hot oven.

BUTTERMILK MUFFINS.

Stir two beaten eggs into one quart of buttermilk; add flour to make batter, one small tablespoon salt, and, lastly, one teaspoon soda dissolved in hot water; bake immediately in a hot oven.

BAKING-POWDER MUFFINS.

Sift three teaspoons baking powder into three pints of flour; put with one quart of milk two beaten eggs, and then add the flour; bake in gem pans or muffin rings in hot oven.

MUFFINS.

One pint sour milk, effervescing with small teaspoon soda, two beaten eggs, one tablespoon melted lard, and flour to make like pound-cake batter.

MUFFINS.
Miss Minnie Wagoner.

One cup sweet milk, three cups flour, one egg, one tablespoon melted butter, one tablespoon sugar and three even teaspoons of baking powder.

CINNAMON MUFFINS.

One cup sugar, one cup sour milk, small teaspoon soda, one egg, one tablespoon cinnamon; add flour for stiff batter, and bake immediately in gem pans.

GRAHAM MUFFINS.
Miss Georgia Howell.

Three cups graham flour, one cup white flour, one quart milk, three-fourths cup yeast, one tablespoon lard, one teaspoon salt, two tablespoons sugar. Let rise.

GRAHAM MUFFINS.

One egg, one tablespoon lard or butter, three cups graham flour, three teaspoons baking-powder, one teaspoon salt; to be mixed with milk or milk and water.

GRAHAM GEMS.
Miss Letta Griffith.

One egg, three cups graham flour, one teaspoon salt, one tablespoon sugar, two teaspoons baking-powder in flour; mix with milk. Have gem pans hot, and when put in oven use only the upper slide.

GRAHAM GEMS No. 1.

One egg, one-half pint sweet milk, one pint graham flour, one teaspoon salt. Heat the gem pans before filling.

MINNESOTA GEMS No. 2.
Mrs. Sam Merrill.

One pint sour milk, one-half teaspoon soda, one egg, one spoonful sugar, one pinch salt, enough graham flour to make stiff batter. Have pans hot and buttered, and the oven hot, so that the gems will begin to bake at once.

GRAHAM GEMS No. 3.
Miss Lida Wheat.

One quart graham flour, one tablespoon sugar, one tablespoon butter, sweet milk to make a thick batter, two and one-half teaspoons-baking powder in the flour; bake quickly.

WATER GEMS.
Mrs. Mary Bernard.

Beat in the air (that it may be aerated) three cups graham flour and a little salt into a stiff batter of the flour and water. Grease and heat your gem pans very hot, and if baked in a quick oven the gems will be very light.

RICE MUFFINS.
Mrs. Enos.

One cup boiled rice, one teaspoon butter, one teaspoon salt, two eggs, one cup milk, flour to make stiff batter to drop from spoon; add to the flour two teaspoons baking-powder. Bake in gem pans.

CORN BREAD.
Mrs. Reynolds.

One egg, one tablespoon melted lard, one teaspoon baking-powder, in three teacups corn meal. Add milk.

CORN BREAD.

One pint sour milk, one pint corn meal, one half-pint white flour, one teaspoon soda, one tablespoon salt, one teaspoon molasses.

CORN BREAD.
Mrs. Ella Miller.

One pint corn meal, one pint buttermilk, one egg, one teaspoon soda, one tablespoon salt.

NONPAREIL CORN BREAD.
Marion Harland.

Two heaping cups Indian meal, one cup flour, three eggs, two and one-half cups milk, one tablespoon lard, two tablespoons white sugar, three teaspoons baking-powder, one teaspoon salt. Beat the eggs very thoroughly, whites and yolks separately; melt the lard.

RICE CORN BREAD.
Mrs. Sappington.

One cup rice boiled soft, three eggs beaten light, one tablespoon melted lard, one pint corn meal, milk to make a thin batter, one tablespoon baking-powder. If sour milk is used, one teaspoon soda.

STEAMED CORN BREAD.
Mrs. Bugbee.

Two cups sour milk, one teaspoon soda, one tablespoon butter, one egg, one teaspoon salt, and corn meal to make dough consistency of pound-cake. Pour in mold and steam two hours.

RISEN CORN BREAD.

Two cups bread sponge, one pint corn meal, two tablespoons molasses, one of sugar, one teaspoon soda, one tablespoon lard; make a stiff batter; put to rise in greased pan. Bake one hour.

CORN MEAL MUFFINS.
Miss Lida Wheat.

Two eggs, one tablespoon melted butter or lard, one pint corn meal; make up with sour milk, in which dissolve one teaspoon soda; have gem pan, muffin rings, or pan, hot and well greased. Bake twenty minutes.

RISEN CORN MEAL MUFFINS.

Scald one cup meal with one pint milk, add butter size of an egg, one table spoon sugar, one egg, one-half cup yeast; flour for stiff batter. When risen, bake in quick oven.

KENTUCKY CORN MEAL PONE.

One quart corn meal, one tablespoon salt, one tablespoon melted lard, cold water for soft dough.

CORN DODGERS.

Same as corn meal pone, only, sugar added and the mixture thinner.

JOHNNY CAKE.

Corn meal, cold water and salt; the cake patted with the hands, and baked on boards before the fire.

YEAST WAFFLES.

Three pints flour, three pints of milk, five eggs, salt, and one-half cup yeast. Warm the milk, with two tablespoons butter in it. Add five eggs well beaten, one teaspoon salt and three pints flour. Lastly, one-half cup yeast. Make them in the evening, and bake next morning.

SOUR-MILK WAFFLES.
Mrs. Spahr, Sr.

One quart sour milk, three tablespoons mixed butter and lard, three eggs beaten separately, one teaspoon soda, one teaspoon salt, and flour to make thick batter.

BAKING-POWDER WAFFLES.

Beat three eggs separately. Add the yolks to one quart of milk, one tablespoon lard and butter, one teaspoon salt, two teaspoons baking-powder sifted in flour enough to make rather a stiff batter.

RICE WAFFLES.
Mrs. Enos.

One teacup boiled rice, two tablespoons butter, three eggs. Sift three teaspoons baking powder into two cups flour. Just before putting into the waffle irons, add the beaten whites of the eggs.

RICE CROQUETTES.

One teacup rice, one pint milk, one pint water, a little salt. Butter a tin pan. Put in the rice, milk and water to swell on the stove. When dry, add two beaten eggs, two tablespoon sugar, and one tablespoon butter. Roll the rice balls in cracker crumbs and fry brown in hot lard.

BUNS.
Mrs. John Rubush.

Make a sponge of one quart flour, one pint milk, and one cup potato yeast. When light, add one cup sugar, one-half cup melted butter, one teaspoon salt and nutmeg. Let this dough rise, and then make into rolls. Let these fit close together, as though round balls. When baked, brush them over with white of an egg beaten stiff with white sugar.

POTATO BUNS.
Mrs. Enos.

One pint mashed potatoes, one pound white sugar, four eggs, one cup yeast, one cup melted butter. Flour enough to make buns of stiff dough.

BUNS.
Miss Miller.

One tablespoon lard and butter, one cup sugar, one cup potato yeast, two eggs, one-half nutmeg. Flour, with one pint milk, one teaspoon salt, one cup raisins or currants. Make of these ingredients a loaf, and when raised, put it into a cake pan. Set to rise, before baking.

PUFFS.
Mrs. Patton.

Two eggs beaten separately, two cups milk, two cups flour, one tablespoon butter. Drop into hot gem pans.

MIXED MUFFINS.
Mrs. Reakirt.

One teacup corn meal, one pint flour, one tablespoon baking-powder, two tablespoons molasses, one of melted lard, one-half teaspoon salt.

OAT-MEAL CAKES.

One cup oat meal, one teaspoon sugar, one cup flour, one teaspoon baking-powder. Add cold water to make batter; beat well and bake immediately.

PARSNIP FRITTERS.

One-half cup milk, one tablespoon butter. Boil parsnips until tender; mash; add two eggs, flour and salt; fry brown.

HOMINY FRITTERS.

To one quart of boiled hominy add one egg, two tablespoons milk and one of flour. Season with pepper and salt; make into cakes and fry in hot lard.

SQUASH CAKES.

Two eggs, one cup cooked squash, one and one-half pints milk, salt, flour to make proper consistency for frying in hot lard.

FUNNEL CAKES.
Miss Miller.

One quart flour, one teaspoon salt, two teaspoons baking-powder, one pint warm milk, three eggs beaten separately. Run this batter through a funnel into hot lard, beginning in the center and running round and round in rings.

SNOW CAKES.
Mrs. Enos.

Make a batter of milk, flour, and a little salt; add new-fallen snow, and immediately drop the batter, in spoonfuls, into the hot lard. The snow causes them to be aerated.

CUCUMBER CAKES OR FRITTERS.

Peel, slice, and cook in a little water, four large cucumbers; mash, and season with pepper and salt; add beaten eggs and flour for batter. Fry in hot lard.

APPLE FRITTERS.
Mrs. Patton.

Chop apples as for mince-meat, and put them in a batter made of two cups flour, teaspoon baking-powder, two eggs beaten separately, one tablespoon sugar, one teaspoon salt, and one cup warm milk. This same recipe can be used when sliced apples are substituted for chopped apples. Peaches can be substituted for apples, making peach fritters.

CLAM FRITTERS.

Chop clams very fine; in the batter of flour, eggs and milk, add the clam liquid.

OYSTER FRITTERS.
Mrs. J. F. Moore, Vincennes.

Make a batter of two eggs, two cups flour, and milk or water; put one oyster to one spoonful of batter. Cove oysters can be used.

GRAHAM-FLOUR BATTER CAKES.

One pint milk, two eggs, one quart graham flour, in which two teaspoons baking-powder have been sifted, one teaspoon salt; if sour milk is used, one-half teaspoon soda.

MUSH.
Mrs. Spahr.

Either graham flour, oat meal or corn meal can be used. Put water in kettle to boil; when boiling stir in the meal by the handful gradually, or by smoothing corn meal with cold water and putting into the boiling water; cook well before adding milk. When cold it can be fried in slices. The milk causes it to brown nicely.

FLANNEL CAKES.

One pint milk, one-half cup yeast, one teaspoon salt, two eggs, one tablespoon melted butter. Make, and set to rise at night, and bake for breakfast.

EGGLESS FLANNEL CAKES.

One quart milk, one-half teacup yeast, one cup corn meal, two cups flour, one tablespoon melted lard, and one teaspoon salt. Scald the corn meal, add milk, then flour and yeast, and set to rise.

BUCKWHEAT CAKES.
Mrs. Patton.

One pint warm water, five cups buckwheat flour, one cup yeast, and one tablespoon sugar or molasses. Make a thin batter. If sour in the morning, add a little soda.

BUCKWHEAT CAKES.

Sift two teaspoons baking-powder in one quart buckwheat flour, one-half pint corn meal, one tablespoon salt, two tablespoons New Orleans molasses. Water to make batter.

CORN CAKES.
Miss Lida Wheat.

Scald one pint corn meal, add one cup flour, two eggs beaten separately, tablespoon salt, one teaspoon baking-powder in the flour, and thin with milk. Do not beat the batter after adding the whites of the eggs, or it will be tough. If sour milk is preferred, one teaspoon of soda, instead of baking-powder.

RICE CAKES.

One cup boiled rice, one teacup salt, one pint milk, three eggs beaten well, and flour to make thin batter, with one teaspoon baking-powder in the flour. Bake on griddle.

BATTER CAKES.
Mrs. Patton.

One quart flour, one tablespoon shortening, teaspoon salt, three eggs beaten separately, milk to make thin batter. With sweet milk, use two teaspoons baking-powder. With sour milk, use one teaspoon soda.

BREAD CAKES.
Mrs. Ella Miller.

Break up stale bread and soak in milk. When perfectly soft, add one-half cup flour, three eggs well beaten, one teaspoon salt. If needed, more milk can be added.

RIPE TOMATO CAKES.

Make a batter of two eggs, flour and water. Slice large ripe tomatoes, cover with the batter, and fry in hot lard. Season with pepper and salt.

GREEN TOMATO CAKES.
Mrs. Black.

Fry slices of green tomatoes dipped in flour and seasoned with salt and pepper. These are a very nice breakfast dish.

GREEN CORN CAKES.
Mrs. Enos.

One dozen ears of corn, three eggs. Grate the corn. Beat the eggs separately. Add the eggs with a teaspoon of butter to the grated corn. Season with pepper and salt. Fry in hot lard and butter. If the batter is too thin, add one tablespoon of flour.

CORN MEAL BANNOCKS.

Scald thoroughly one pint corn meal. Add salt and one egg, cream and melted butter. Make into balls, and fry in hot lard, turning them from side to side.

VANITIES.
Mrs. Enos.

Beat two eggs, with little salt, teaspoon rose water, and flour in which one teaspoon baking-powder has been sifted, and roll out. Cut with a cake cutter, fry in hot lard, sift powdered sugar over them while hot, and when cool put a teaspoon of jelly in the center of each. Nice for tea or dessert.

BAKING-POWDER BISCUIT.
Mrs. Lowe.

Sift together one quart of flour and three teaspoons baking-powder; add one tablespoon salt and one tablespoon lard, either melted or distributed over the flour in small pieces; wet the flour with sweet milk and roll one-half inch thick; cut with biscuit cutter and bake in five minutes. Milk is better than water in biscuit, but if you have not milk add more lard or butter and use water.

SODA BISCUIT.
Mrs. Patton.

Rub into one quart of flour two teaspoons cream tartar and one of soda, two tablespoons lard, one tablespoon salt; moisten with sweet milk.

VIENNA BISCUIT.

Add to one quart flour three teaspoons baking-powder and a tablespoonful of butter; mix with sweet milk, roll a half-inch thick, butter and fold over, and moisten on top with milk to give them a gloss.

BUTTERMILK BISCUIT.
Miss Bugbee.

Make a soft dough; one pint buttermilk, one teaspoon soda, two teaspoons melted butter. The soda may be sifted with the flour or dissolved in the buttermilk.

BEAT BISCUIT.

Rub four tablespoons butter into one quart flour; beat two eggs light and put them into one teacup milk; stir the milk and eggs into the flour; add salt; mold, knead, pound, roll thin and bake fifteen minutes.

BAKING-POWDER BISCUIT.
Mrs. Sappington.

One quart flour, one tablespoon baking-powder mixed through the flour; add one even tablespoon of salt and rub in one tablespoon lard; mix very soft with sweet milk or sweet buttermilk; knead as little as possible and bake in a quick oven.

TO FRESHEN CRACKERS, BISCUIT, ROLLS, Etc.

Dip in water and put in hot oven.

CRACKER TOAST.

Butter the crackers, lay them in a bread pan and sprinkle lightly with salt; put milk over them and place in the oven to heat thoroughly.

KENTUCKY BEAT BISCUIT.
Mrs. Rev. Brown, Madison, Ind.

One quart flour, one tablespoon lard and sufficient salt, mixed thoroughly. Make this into a very stiff dough, with equal portions of water and sweet milk; beat or work with a machine until the dough blisters and shines like satin; roll out moderately thin and stick with fork several times; bake in moderate oven until thoroughly done.

BROWN BREAD.
Mrs. Hope.

Two cups corn meal, two cups graham flour, one cup molasses, one teaspoon soda, one of salt; mix well and boil three hours.

CORN PONE.
Mrs. Hope.

One quart buttermilk, two teaspoons soda, one quart meal, two cups flour, one cup syrup, one tablespoon salt; bake three hours in a crock with skillet turned over the top; after removing from oven keep skillet on till cool.

SOUPS, Etc.

CELERY SOUP.
Mrs. John Alling, Chicago.

Three pints of chicken broth, one small cup of rice, one quart of milk, three or four stalks of celery. Cook the rice in the milk until very soft; then add the chicken broth, into which you have cut up the celery. Let it boil a few minutes, strain through a collander, season with salt and pepper and serve hot.

BEEF SOUP.
Mrs. Springer.

Put on a soup bone. Let the shank be covered with water and be kept simmering for several hours. For dinner it should be put on at early breakfast time. A sirloin steak is good if bones are used as well as the lean meat. All soup meat should be put on in cold water. When a scum is formed it should be taken off. Soups may vary, by having beef as the base, with a variety of vegetables, or fried bread, or noodles, or herbs, or rice, or pearl barley, or spices. Vegetables should be sliced. Potatoes, turnips, parsnips, carrots, cabbage, tomatoes, onions or celery may be used. Salt should be put in at the last, also catsup, if desired. If the soup boils at all it should be just before taken up, so that the vegetables may be tender.

VEAL SOUP.
Mrs. Enos.

A knuckle of veal, boiled until the meat falls from the bone. Onions sliced should be put on with the meat. When the meat is boiled take out the bones and add sliced potatoes to the meat and soup; season with pepper, salt, a little cloves, sweet marjorem and a little coriander seed, pounded; make dumplings as biscuit dough, with the addition of an egg; roll them in round balls or cut them in squares; lastly, add chopped hard-boiled eggs.

MUTTON SOUP.

A leg of mutton, boiled three hours. After seasoning with salt and pepper boil quickly a dropped batter made of one egg, milk and flour.

OYSTER SOUP.

For one quart of oysters use one pint of water and one quart of new milk; thicken, though not very thick, with rolled crackers; season with butter, pepper and salt. The oysters should not be added until the milk is boiling hot, and the whole should then boil quickly.

NOODLE SOUP.
Mrs. Enos.

Boil a chicken until tender; add an onion. Make noodles by taking three eggs and working into them flour enough to make stiff to roll; when dry enough to fold, roll them over and over; cut slices from the ends; put these into the soup and season.

POTATO SOUP.

Slice the potatoes; put them on the stove in sufficient water; season with pepper, salt and butter; add milk or cream thickened with flour. If desired, add chopped hard-boiled eggs.

CORN SOUP.

Boil shank of beef for two hours; add salt, tomatoes, corn cut from the cob, one quart of milk, lump of butter size of an egg, pepper and powdered crackers.

BEAN SOUP.

To one quart of beans take two quarts of water; boil the beans until they will mash soft. Mutton, beef or pork seasons the soup. Butter and flour rubbed together are a substitute for meat. Put toasted bread into the soup tureen.

PEA SOUP.

Boil peas slowly in a little water; add milk and crackers, either rolled or broken; season with pepper, salt and butter.

TOMATO SOUP.
Miss Georgie Howell.

One quart ripe tomatoes; boil slowly one-half hour; strain, season with salt, pepper and butter to taste; to this add one-half gallon boiling milk, stirring all the time; add four crackers, rolled or grated fine. Serve immediately.

TIT-BIT SOUP.

One pound chicken or turkey, cut fine; cook till tender; pick and chop; put back in broth; season with salt, pepper, butter and a little celery; boil fifteen minutes. When ready to serve add one-half gallon boiling milk and two well-beaten eggs.

POTATO SOUP.
Rev. Aaron Miller.

Boil peeled potatoes until they will mash; slice light wheat bread of equal quantity; stir this with the potatoes in melted butter or rich cream, then boil in rich milk until thick as mush, adding salt.

FISH.

BAKED FISH.
Mrs. Craig.

For a three-pound fish, clean nicely, salt and pepper, and roll in flour; fill with dressing as for chicken; Tie and lay the fish in a pan previously heated and buttered. Wooden pins or a saucer may be used to brace the fish from the bottom of the pan; bake two and one-half hours; serve with melted butter.

BOILED FISH.
Miss Corson.

Place over the fire in plenty of cold, salted water; bring slowly to the boiling point; keep the water boiling until the fins can be pulled from the fish. Salmon, the finest of all fish for boiling, is excellent with a dish of buttered green peas in summer.

EGG SAUCE FOR FISH.
Mrs. Sappington, Madison.

Boil four eggs ten minutes. To prevent their turning blue dip them in cold water; peel and chop fine; stir in a large tablespoon butter and a cup of cream.

SALMON IN A MOLD.
Mrs. Foltz.

One can salmon, four eggs beaten light, four tablespoons melted butter, one-half cup fine bread crumbs. Season with pepper and salt; chop the fish fine and rub it in a bowl with the back of a silver spoon, adding the butter until it is a smooth paste; add the crumbs to the eggs, and season before mixing all together; put into a buttered pudding mold, and boil or steam for an hour.

SAUCE.

One cup milk heated and thickened with one tablespoon corn starch, the liquor from the canned salmon, one large spoon butter, one raw egg, one teaspoon mushroom or tomato catsup, one pinch mace and one cayenne. Put the egg in last; boil one minute, and when the salmon is turned out, pour over it.

BAKED HALIBUT.
Mrs. Foltz.

Take a piece of halibut weighing five or six pounds and lay it in salt water for two hours; wipe dry and cut the skin; set in a baking-tin in a hot oven, basting often with butter and water, heating in a tin; bake one hour, or until a fork will penetrate; take the gravy in the pan; add water if needed; stir in a tablespoon of walnut catsup, a teaspoon of Worcester sauce and the juice of a lemon; thicken with brown flour wet up with cold water; boil up once and put in a sauce boat. Halibut, salmon, herring and other dried fish can be heated through by quickly turning from side to side in hot frying-pan, or they may be broiled.

LOBSTER CUTLETS.

One-half pound canned lobsters, one ounce flour, one ounce butter, one gill cold water, a little salt and pepper, a few drops lemon juice, and two or three tablespoons bread crumbs. Cut up into pieces the meat from the can; melt the butter; add the flour and cold water; stir until the mixture boils; add the meat. When cold, form into small cutlets, roll them in egg and then in bread crumbs. Fry them in hot lard.

BAKED LOBSTER.
Mrs. Bently.

Chop the meat, mix bread crumbs with it, and add a dressing of butter, cayenne pepper, a little vinegar, and

W. H. ALLEN & CO.,
DRUGGISTS,

Headquarters for anything in Drug Line,

Fine Perfumes, Toilet Articles, Soaps, Etc.

Cor. Pennsylvania & Market Sts, opp. Post Office,

INDIANAPOLIS, IND.

Jefferson Caylor,

OSAGE  MILL.

DEALER IN

Agricultural Implements,

57 AND 59
WEST WASHINGTON ST.

INDIANAPOLIS, INDIANA.

Correspondence Solicited.

1860. ——— THE ——— 1883.
WASHINGTON

Life Insurance Company,
OF NEW YORK.

W. A. BREWER, Jr., President.   WM. HAXTON, Secretary.

OFFICE, COAL AND IRON EXCHANGE.

ASSETS, - - - $6,500,000

The motto of the Company has always been, that "SAFETY and SUCCESS must always go hand in hand;" hence, its policy is first to do a SAFE, afterwards a LARGE business.

Its Investments are the very best that can be obtained, and its management has never been questioned.

The great and distinguishing feature of the **WASHINGTON** is its **NON-FORFEITABLE DIVIDENDS.**

A policy in the **WASHINGTON** can not lapse by **NON-PAYMENT** of premium so long as there are any dividends, or accumulation of dividends remaining to its credit

Thereby **HOLDING POLICIES** in force by their **AUTOMATIC** principle, whether premium be paid when due or not, and preventing lapse by **ACCIDENT, CARELESSNESS, or INABILITY** to pay.

Giving Policy Holders the right to renew their insurance at the expiration of the dividend holding period, without a new Medical Examination.

ITS POLICIES are the most liberal issued by any Company.

ITS CONTRACT is in **PLAIN, CONCISE** language, contains fewer restrictions than any other Company.

This Company has a reputation, fairly won, and a character, firmly established, the foundation of which was laid in a charter wherein the rights of its policy holders were made secure, and in the adoption of plans of insurance that have made a policy granted by this Company a most desirable possession. * * * We know of no Company that we can more cordially recommend to the public than the Washington Life Insurance Company of this city.—[New York Christian Advocate.

J. D. SUTTON, State Agent,
INDIANAPOLIS, IND.

DR. S. L. FULLER,   **M. M. CUMMINGS,**
Gen'l Agt. Michigan, Wisconsin & Indiana,   Special Agent.
Detroit, Mich.

A Necessity in Every Well-Ordered Household!

THE GATE CITY STONE FILTER.

C is the cooler; *c* its cover; *F* the filter; *i* the perforated ice shelf; *s* the filtering stone, and *L* the ice on the shelf.

The only FILTER IN THE WORLD that will insure

Perfectly Pure Water.

Yellow Fever, Typhoid Fever, Bright's Disease, and a very large proportion of the "thousand and one diseases that flesh is heir to" are produced by the use of

IMPURE WATER.

The "Gate City" filters the *water slowly* through a natural stone and not only removes all the animalculæ, sand, clay, etc., but as proven by microscopic and chemical analysis, also removes all chlorine, albuminoids, ammonia and organic matter, which are the disease breeding elements of ordinary drinking water, leaving the water entirely clear, sparkling and colorless. Prices less than other filters of equal capacity. Write for pamphlet and prices.

REFERENCES—The Indiana State Board of Health, Indianapolis Board of Health, and thousands of well-known physicians and chemists throughout the United States.

Address,

GEO. B. WRIGHT & CO.
31 West Market St., Indianapolis.

I. L. FRANKEM,
34 E. WASHINGTON STREET,
AGENT FOR

OVER 500,000   NOW IN USE.

HULL'S VAPOR COOK STOVE.

You can bake, broil, fry or stew on them to perfection. For summer use they are unexcelled. Warranted to give perfect satisfaction.

N. B.—Don't fail to get the Hull Burner.

F. M. TAGUE'S
Shirt Factory and Steam Laundry,

SHIRTS— Workmanship and Perfect Fit guaranteed.

LAUNDRYING Collars and Cuffs a specialty. Equal to Troy work.

74 N. PENNSYLVANIA ST., INDIANAPOLIS.

the yolks of three hard-boiled eggs. Put this into a dish, and over the top put a few bread crumbs and bits of butter; bake until brown. It may be eaten hot or cold.

CODFISH BALLS.

Wash, soak, and boil one-half hour; pick to pieces and take away the bone: mix the minced meat with mashed potatoes and fry the balls.

SPICED MACKEREL.
Mrs. Black.

Let it boil fifteen minutes, then pour on it boiling vinegar, pepper, salt and spices. Serve cold.

MAYONAISE DRESSING.
Mrs. Clough.

Mix the yolks of two eggs with one cup of sweet oil; add one teaspoon mixed mustard, two teaspoons salt and one of sugar.

OYSTERS.

OYSTER STEW.

One pint milk, one pint water, one-half can oysters, six rolled crackers, pepper, salt and butter. Put in the oysters when the milk and water have come to a boil. When boiled up once, remove.

FRIED OYSTERS.

Roll the oysters in corn meal and fry in hot lard. They may be dipped in rolled cracker, and then in egg, before frying; or, for fritters, they may be dipped in batter, and fried.

PICKLED OYSTERS.

Let cook slowly a few minutes; then put in a jar, covering with spices and hot vinegar.

ESCOLLOPED OYSTERS.

Cover a well buttered dish with a layer of broken cracker—above this, with oysters—and so continue until the dish or pan is filled. Let cracker be the top layer. Season with butter, pepper and salt.

OYSTER PIE.

Line a dish with plain pastry. Fill with oysters and bread or cracker crumbs. Cover with the pastry, and bake quickly.

SWEET-BREAD AND OYSTER PIE.
Mrs. Binford.

Stew the sweet-breads until tender; have a dish lined with a good paste. Cut the sweet-breads up in small pieces. Put in a dish with the oysters, pepper, salt, tablespoon of butter, and yolks of three eggs boiled hard and mashed fine. Another layer of oysters and sweet-bread until the dish is full. Put on a top crust and bake.

OYSTER SALAD.
Mrs. Clough.

Cut up one-quart can of cove oysters. Make a dressing of the beaten yolks of three eggs and one cup of vinegar. Add one tablespoon butter, with mustard, pepper, salt and celery seed to taste. Put this dressing on the stove, and stir all the time to prevent lumping; let it boil until thick, and when cold pour over the oysters, and mix well.

MACARONI AND OYSTERS.

Boil the macaroni, and alternate layers of it with oysters. Put bread crumbs as top layer, and pour over all a broth made of milk and the oyster liquor. Season with pepper, salt and butter.

MEATS, Etc.

MOCK DUCK.
Mrs. Enos.
Either a flank or a round beef steak, with a dressing made of bread and onions, seasoned with pepper, salt and butter. Spread the dressing over the steak, roll up the steak and bake.

HAM TOAST.
Mince cooked ham; add pepper and mustard. Beat up egg and mix, adding sufficient milk to moisten, before heating. Serve on toast or fried bread.

LAMB STEAKS.
Dip them in egg and then in bread crumbs. Fry until brown.

PORK FRITTERS.
After frying a slice of pork, dip other slices into a batter made of corn meal and flour. Fry them in the hot fat; season with salt and pepper; cook until light brown.

BOILED HAM.
Mrs. Hereth.
Wash and scrape the ham. Put on a kettle large enough to cover the ham with water. When the water is at the boiling point, put in the ham. For every pound of ham, allow fifteen minutes' boiling.

ROAST BEEF.
Put in a pan with a little depth of water, after rubbing over it salt and pepper. Baste frequently, by pouring the water from a spoon over it. Fifteen minutes to every pound of beef will cook it.

PRESSED BEEF.
Mrs. Rubush.

Get a flank of beef. Boil it until it is real tender. Take out all the bone and gristle. Season with salt and pepper, put it into a crock, put on it a plate with a weight to press it down. Serve in slices.

PRESSED CHICKEN.

Prepare as above. Salt while cooking.

SMOTHERED SPRING CHICKEN.
Mrs. Kellog.

Cut open in the back, wash clean and put in a pan; season with butter, pepper and salt; put in a hot oven and bake half an hour; dredge with flour; baste frequently.

CHICKEN PIE.
Mrs. Black.

Make dough as for biscuit. Stew the chicken thoroughly, and pour the gravy upon slices of potato and the pieces of chicken, after lining a deep pan with the dough and putting in the chicken and potato in alternate layers; dredge with flour and season; spread over an upper crust. Let both upper and lower crust be cut, that the air as well as the gravy may pass back and forth.

ROAST VEAL.
Mrs. Kellog.

Prepare the breast of veal for dressing; then take one quart dry bread crumbs or rolled crackers, the yelks of two eggs, one tablespoon powdered sage, one-half cup butter; rub all together; split the veal and put in the dressing. Bake in a moderate oven, basting frequently.

VEAL LOAF.
Mrs. J. F. Moore, Vincennes.

A cold roast of veal chopped fine, one cup bread crumbs, a lemon rind, two beaten eggs, season well, according to taste; mix and make into a loaf; cover with beaten egg and sprinkle on bread crumbs; bake half an hour. Slice when cold.

FOR CURING MEAT.

One gallon water, one and one-half pounds salt, one-half pound sugar, one-half ounce saltpeter, one-fourth ounce potash; boil together until ready to skim; pour out to cool. When cold pour over the beef, to remain four or five weeks. The meat should not be put down for two days after killing. Let it be slightly sprinkled during that time with powdered saltpeter, to remove the surface blood.

LARD.

Skin the leaf lard, or, if careful to stir, it may be cut into inch pieces without skinning. Put a little water into the kettle and melt the lard in it slowly. Boil until clear. Strain through a cloth or sieve.

SAUSAGE.

Take tenderloin or mixed fat and lean pork; season, after chopping fine, with powdered sage, black pepper, salt, and spices, if desired.

MEAT PUFFS.
Mrs. Enos.

Take cold meat of any kind; cut it into small bits; season with pepper and salt; mash some potatoes and make into paste with two eggs; roll out with a dust of flour; cut with a large biscuit cutter; turn over one half, inclosing a layer of meat, and pinch edges together; fry in butter and lard.

EGG AND APPLE OMELETTE.
Marion Harland.

Six large pippins, one tablespoon butter, three eggs, five or six tablespoons sugar, nutmeg and rose water. Stew the apples, beat them smooth, adding the butter, sugar and nutmeg. When cold, put with eggs, beaten separately. Pour into a buttered baking dish. Bake, until a delicate brown. Eat warm.

HAM OMELETTE.

Beat six eggs light, separately. Add to the yolks, one cup milk; pepper and salt. Stir in the whites. Have heated in frying pan a lump of butter. Pour in the mixture. Slip the knife under often to prevent burning. When done, scatter over it chopped ham.

SOUTHERN VEAL STEW.
Mrs. Basore, Broadway, Virginia.

Peel and boil one-half dozen onions, drain and slice them; have ready two pounds nice sliced veal; put in a stew-pan; season with salt and a little cayenne; cover the veal with the onions, and some sliced Irish potatoes; lay on them some bits of fresh butter, rolled in flour; put in a very little lemon, just as it is done. Lamb, chicken, squirrel or rabbit are equally nice.

CROQUETTS.

Chop fresh meat fine; roll dried bread with it, also crumbled fine; add salt, pepper and cloves, with one egg; work all together and make into balls the size of an egg; roll in bread crumbs and egg; fry in hot lard; dish with gravy flavored with walnut catsup.

EGG HASH.

Take cold veal and chop it fine; put butter with it in a pan; sprinkle in it a little flour; brown it; boil a few eggs and add to this veal; season with pepper and salt.

VEAL HASH.

Chop cold veal and add mashed potatoes; make into cakes; season with pepper and salt, and fry.

SCRAPPLE.

Use hogshead or feet, or any part of pork; boil until the meat falls from the bones; take out of the pot and return the meat, only; season with pepper and salt, sweet marjorem and a little coriander seed; thicken with corn meal or buckwheat. When cold, cut in slices and fry.

VEAL ROLL.
Mrs. Isaac Pattison.

Two pounds veal chopped fine, two eggs, one tablespoon salt, six crackers rolled fine, one tablespoon melted butter, one-half pound pickled pork, one teaspoon pepper. Bake in a loaf one hour.

IRISH STEW.

Two pounds potatoes peeled, sliced and parboiled, two pounds mutton chops, two pounds beef, six onions sliced, a slice of ham or lean bacon, spoonful of pepper and two of salt. In stewing, let the lowest layer and the topmost be potatoes.

MINCED VEAL.

Mince the slices of roasted veal finely, after trimming off the brown edges; chop one small onion fine; fry it in butter and add three tablespoons of veal gravy. When boiling hot turn in the minced veal. If not moist enough pour in a little boiling water. Serve with poached eggs on the top of it.

BEEF HASH.
Mrs. Bently.

Take cold pieces of beef and chop them fine; add cold boiled potatoes chopped fine; add pepper and salt and a little warm water. Put all in a frying pan and cook slowly twenty minutes.

DRY BEEF HASH.

Made as above, omitting water and substituting mashed potatoes; pound together in a stone crock; cut in slices and fry in hot lard or butter.

CORN BEEF HASH.

Season with salt and pepper, chop fine, and to one-third meat add two-thirds chopped cold boiled potatoes, and one onion chopped fine. Place in dripping pan, pour water in at sides, and dredge the top with flour. When the flour has browned, take out, add a lump of butter, stir it through several times.

BEEF LIVER.

Fry slices of salt pork; take them out, and fry slices of liver in the fat. Thicken the gravy with flour and water, mixed smooth. Pepper and salt.

MUTTON CUTLETS.
Mrs. Bently.

Cut from the end of a neck of mutton, making the slices one-half an inch thick. Pepper, salt, and boil over a brisk fire.

VEAL CUTLETS.

Fry slowly to a delicate brown.

BROILED BEEFSTEAK.

Broil on griddle, not turning until the side is done. Season, after taking up, with much butter and pepper.

FRIED BEEFSTEAK.

Put into a very hot frying-pan; turn often; season before taking up.

FRIED BEEFSTEAK WITH GRAVY.

Put into boiling lard in frying pan. When done, stir in smoothly water or milk, with flour. Salt and pepper.

ITALIAN CHEESE.
Mrs. Foltz.

Cover a knuckle of veal with two quarts of water. Boil until tender; then strip the meat from the bone, and let it cool. Cut into small pieces, strain the liquor, and return all to the kettle. Season with a scant teaspoon of cloves, and the same of ground allspice; salt to taste. Boil until it jellies; then turn into a mold which has been lined with hard boiled eggs, cut into thin slices. When cold, turn out and slice after it is put on the table.

VEAL MARBLE.
Mrs. Foltz.

Boil a beef tongue the day before it is to be used, and the same number of pounds of lean veal; chop very fine, keeping them in separate vessels. Season the tongue with pepper, a teaspoon of made mustard, a little nutmeg, and cloves; the veal, in like manner, adding salt. Pack in alternate spoonsful in bowls or jars which have been buttered; press very hard; cover with melted butter, if you wish to keep it several days. Turn out whole, and cut in thin slices for tea.

FRIED CHICKEN.
Mrs. Binford.

If a year old, parboil it before frying: let the pieces be cut and the legs especially be stripped of their meat; spread out these pieces that all may be fried evenly. It is the Chinese way, and superior. Season with salt and pepper and dredge with flour before putting into the hot lard.

CHICKEN CROQUETTES.
Mrs. Clough.

To a cup full of chopped chicken add a tablespoonful of milk, a well-beaten egg, a little salt and pepper: fry the mixture in little cakes, a tablespoonful in each, browning nicely on both sides. They may be flavored with celery seed.

PRESSED BEEF.
Mrs. Will Siddall.

Boil seven pounds—a neck piece—until the bone slips out; boil the liquor down to one pint; chop the beef, add the liquor, set on fire and season with salt, pepper, sage, summer savory, nutmeg, and butter the size of an egg; beat thoroughly, put in a tin pan and press down with a weight for twenty-four hours.

SANDWICHES.

Butter thin slices of bread; spread lightly with mustard; put between them thin slices of beef, ham, tongue, or fried oysters.

HOW TO CORN BEEF.
Mrs. Dr. Gillette.

To one gallon water add two pounds salt, one-third pound sugar, one-half ounce saltpetre. Boil, skim well, and when cool pour over the beef.

BEEF CROQUETTES.
Mrs. Etta Reakirt.

One and one-half pounds lean beef; chop finely; add one coffee cup of finely rolled cracker, and a small lump of butter; melt, season with salt and pepper and the least dust of sage; take two or three beaten eggs and mix all together into a loaf. Bake for two-thirds of an hour.

STUFFING OR DRESSING.
Mrs. Black.

Soak in milk or water pieces of bread; season with pepper, salt and a little sage. Oysters can be added to bread crumbs or powdered crackers, by chopping fine, adding butter and the oyster liquor.

TO ROAST TURKEY OR OTHER FOWL.

Wash clean; fill with dressing; dredge with flour and a little salt and pepper; put in the pan with a depth of two inches of water; baste frequently by taking the water in a spoon and pouring over the fowl; put balls of dressing in the pan.

TURKEY DRESSING.
Mrs. Springer.

Have butter hot in a skillet; put in it squares of bread. When they brown, pour over them oyster liquor, or milk, or water. Season and use.

TONGUE.

Beef tongue should be boiled one hour; after cooling, the outside skin should be peeled. Serve in thin slices.

EGGS.

BOILED EGGS.

Three minutes or less time is ordinarily given to boiling. A better way is, to put the eggs in boiling hot water and set them away from the fire. The vessel should be kept covered. In fifteen minutes the eggs will be cooked through evenly.

POACHED OR DROPPED EGGS.

Have enough water in the pans to more than cover the eggs. Break the eggs singly in a saucer and slip them in the water. As soon as they whiten, take them out with a perforated ladle, place each egg on a piece of buttered toast, and sprinkle with salt and pepper.

SCRAMBLED EGGS.

When a tablespoonful of butter, or lard, is hot in the frying pan, pour in the eggs and stir rapidly until sufficiently cooked.

OMELETTE.

Beat three eggs, add two tablespoons each of milk and bread crumbs. Put the mixture into hot butter and fry. Sprinkle with salt and pepper, and roll up like a jelly cake.

OMELETTE.

Eight eggs well beaten, one cup sweet milk, pepper and salt to taste. Make the skillet hot and grease with butter and lard. Pour the mixture in, and when cooked through, quarter and turn. Heat the skillet on front of stove, and change to the back, before cooking the omelette.

FRIED POTATOES WITH EGGS.
Mrs. Enos.

Fry cold potatoes in a little hot lard. When browned, stir in a few eggs. Dish immediately.

EGG BALLS.
Mrs. Reynolds.

Three cups mashed potatoes, one-half cup flour, one-half teacup sweet milk, two well-beaten eggs, a little salt and pepper; shape into balls and fry in boiling lard.

STUFFED EGGS.
Miss Craft.

Boil eggs until the yelks are mealy; peel, and cut into halves, round way. Turn out the yelks; mash them fine, mixing with butter, pepper, salt and vinegar, to suit taste. Return this mixture to the white cup shape of the egg, placing upon the dish. Besides being a good relish, it is a pretty dish for the table.

VEGETABLES, Etc.

TOMATO HASH.

Into a well-buttered dish put a layer of tomatoes, next of sliced meat, then of bread and butter until the dish is full; bake in a hot oven after pouring egg over top of last layer and seasoning.

ESCALLOPED TOMATOES.
Mrs. Binford.

Put in a buttered baking dish a layer of bread crumbs seasoned with bits of butter, then a layer of sliced tomatoes seasoned with salt, pepper, and sugar, if desired, then a layer of crumbs, and so on, finishing with bread crumbs; bake about three-fourths of an hour. Sliced onions may be mixed with the slices of tomato.

FRIED TOMATOES.
Mrs. Patton.

Either green or ripe tomatoes, sliced and rolled in flour; season with pepper and salt, and fry in lard. The slices may be dipped in egg and then in either bread or cracker crumbs before frying.

BROILED TOMATOES.

Broil the slices on a grid-iron; turn them on a hot dish and put over them butter, pepper and salt.

STEWED TOMATOES.
Mrs. Dr. Hester.

Cook quickly and take up; add salt, one teaspoon sugar and one tablespoon butter, mixed with flour.

BAKED TOMATOES AND APPLES.
Mrs. Hereth.

Slice good, ripe tomatoes and Vandever apples; put in a pan alternate layers, with sugar sprinkled over them, and bake slowly one hour. No water is needed.

SLICED TOMATOES.
Mrs. John Rubush.

Scald ripe tomatoes and let them stand in cold water; then take off the skin and slice; serve with salt, pepper and vinegar.

TOMATOES AND CORN.
Mrs. Patton.

Cook together, after stewing separately, one-third corn and two-thirds tomatoes.

STEWED CORN.
Mrs. Reynolds.

Cut off the cobs and boil; season with salt, pepper and butter, or add cream. Cook on the cobs, if preferred.

FRIED CORN.

Fry corn, either with or without potato, and season.

CORN PUDDING.
Mrs. Patton.

Cut down four ears of corn; beat two eggs with one pint of milk, butter size of an egg, three tablespoons flour; add salt and pepper, beat well together and bake one hour. Serve as a vegetable.

SUCCOTASH.
Mrs. Patton.

One pint of green corn cut from the cob and two-thirds of a pint of either Lima or stringed beans; stew in water enough to cover. When tender, season with butter, pepper, salt and a little milk. Cook together a few moments.

LIMA BEANS.

Put on the stove in cold water and boil until tender; season with rich milk, butter, pepper and salt. Let them simmer.

CANNING CORN.
Mrs. Enos.

Boil on the cob until half done, then cut it off, and to twenty-two quarts of corn, use three and one-half ounces of tartaric acid. Boil the corn in a good deal of water. When done, add the acid dissolved in a little warm water.

SOUTHERN GREEN CORN PUDDING.
Mrs. Rev. Brown, Madison.

One dozen ears corn, grated into a buttered pudding dish. Add morning's milk to consistency of thick batter. Season well with butter, pepper and salt, and bake three quarters of an hour.

STRING BEANS.
Mrs. Rubush.

Cut each end and take off the string. Boil from one to two hours. A piece of salt pork may season them, or butter, pepper and salt.

BOSTON BAKED BEANS.
Mrs. Dr. Wiley.

Pick and wash one heaping pint of dressed beans. Put them in a sauce pan with enough cold water to cover them. Let them simmer over the fire until they come to a boil. Drain off the water, and put in a bean pot with half a pound of pork. Pour a little molasses on the top. Let cook slowly for six or eight hours.

BAKED BEANS.
Mrs. Rubush.

Boil the beans and pour off the water. Then put them into a pan with pork that has just been parboiled, and bake them until brown. Season.

GREEN PEAS.
Mrs. Black.

Shell and put into boiling water. They will cook in twenty minutes. Add cream, in seasoning. Broken crackers improve them.

YANKEE BAKED BEANS.
Mrs. Bugbee.

Take one quart of white dried beans, or more if necessary, put them in a vessel with cold water enough to come above the beans two or three inches. Boil them until, when you take up a spoonful and blow them, the skin will crack; then take them out in a cullendar and pour cold water over them to rinse them off; then put them in a brown earthen bean pot. Leave space to put half a pound of pickled or salt pork, mostly fat; one small tablespoon of molasses, a big teaspoon of salt. Then put a thin covering of beans over the pork, and fill up with boiling water As fast as the water dries away, fill up with more boiling water, until they have cooked five or six hours. When done, have them laid away, so they will be moist enough to be nice.

CAULIFLOWER.
Mrs. Ferrell

Wash the flower in salt and water; tie in a floured cloth and boil forty minutes, putting it into salted boiling water. Make a sauce of a small teacup corn starch, smoothed with cold water, and added to one-half pint sweet milk boiled with one cup of the water in which the cauliflower was boiled. Put in a piece of butter as large as an egg, and one teaspoon vinegar. When the butter has melted, pour this sauce over the cauliflower, and serve.

SPINACH.
Mrs. Ferrell.

Pick off the leaves and boil in plenty of hot salted water. Drain; chop upon a board or in a tray; put into a saucepan with a tablespoonful of butter, a little pepper and salt, and a few spoonsful of milk or cream. Stir and heat until bubbling hot; pour out upon small squares of toasted bread.

POTATO CROQUETS.
Mrs. Reakirt.

Eight good sized potatoes, boiled and mashed. Add butter, and season. Beat two eggs, whites and yolks separately. Add one-half cup of flour to the mashed potatoes. Make into balls and fry.

POTATOES AND CAULIFLOWER.

Chop together both when cold, after boiling. Serve hot with a sauce of one cup sweet milk, one cup water, one teaspoon vinegar, and one-half cup butter, boiled together.

SWEET POTATOES.

After steaming, put them in the oven to dry.

POTATOES AND TURNIPS.

Steam, then mash together, add cream, salt and pepper. The potatoes take from the turnips their strong taste, and make them delicate.

TO FRY EGG-PLANT.

Pare and let it lie fifteen minutes in salt and water; wipe dry and dip in rolled cracker, after seasoning with pepper and salt and dipping each piece in the beaten yolk of an egg.

HUBBARD SQUASH.

Cut in round slices, leaving on the peel, and bake in the oven.

CORN OYSTERS.
Miss Kittie Lodge.

One pint grated corn, one teacup flour, one-half teacup butter, one egg, pepper and salt. Fry in lard.

MUSHROOMS.
Mrs. S. E. Wagoner.

Split them and soak in weak salt and water a few hours; flour, and fry in butter to a nice brown.

SALSIFY, OR OYSTER-PLANT.
Mrs. S. E. Wagoner.

Cut, round way, in thin slices; stew in water, and then add milk, butter, pepper and salt, as for oyster-stew.

SQUASH.

Steam and dry before mashing.

ASPARAGUS.

Boil until tender; serve with drawn butter on toast; put over it slices of hard-boiled eggs.

BAKED MACARONI.
Mrs. Reakirt.

Break up one-half pound into small pieces; put in boiling water; stew for twenty minutes; salt; drain well; place a layer in a buttered dish; cover with grated cheese and a few lumps of butter. Alternate in this way, and add one gill of cream or milk. Bake one-half hour.

MASHED POTATOES.
Mrs. Col. Merrill.

Boil the potatoes, but not done. After peeling, put in as little milk as is necessary for mashing the potatoes as light as cake; beat them very hard with a spoon. Season with salt and butter.

KALECANNON.

Boiled cabbage and potatoes in equal proportions as a breakfast dish.

OCHRA.

Wash, cut in half, season and fry.

BEETS.

Young beets boil quickly; but when a little old, they take at least two hours. The skins should not be taken off until after cooking. Young potatoes boiled separately and afterward sliced with the beets, and a dressing of butter or cream, are very nice.

SMOTHERED POTATOES.

Mrs. Enos.

Slice raw potatoes and onions; put them in a frying pan, into hot lard; season with pepper and salt, and cover closely.

POTATO PUFFS.

Mrs. Enos.

Take cold meat of any kind; cut into small bits; season with pepper and salt; mash some potatoes, and make into paste with two eggs; roll out with a dust of flour; cut with a large biscuit cutter; turn over one half, inclosing a layer of meat, and pinch edges together; fry in butter and lard.

RULES FOR COOKING VEGETABLES.

A French cook gives the following general rules for cooking all kinds of vegetables: Green vegetables should be thoroughly washed in cold water, and then dropped into water which has been salted and is beginning to boil. There should be a tablespoonful of salt for each two quarts of water. If the water boils long before the vegetables are put in, it has lost all its gases, and the mineral ingredients are deposited on the bottom and sides of the kettle, so that the water is flat and tasteless, then the vegetables will not look well, nor have a fine flavor. The time for boiling green vegetables depends much upon the age, and time they have been gathered. The younger, and more freshly gathered, the more quickly they are cooked. The following is a very good time-table for cooking vegetables:

Potatoes, boiled, thirty minutes.
Potatoes, baked, forty-five minutes.
Sweet potatoes, boiled, fifty minutes.
Sweet potatoes, baked, sixty minutes.
Squash, boiled, twenty-five minutes.
Green peas, boiled, twenty to forty minutes.
Shelled beans, boiled, sixty minutes.
String beans, boiled, one or two hours.
Green corn, thirty to sixty minutes.
Asparagus, fifteen to thirty minutes.
Spinach, one or two hours.
Tomatoes, fresh, one hour.
Tomatoes, canned, thirty minutes.
Cabbage, forty-five minutes or two hours.
Cauliflower, one or two hours.
Dandelions, two or three hours.
Beet greens, one hour.
Onions, one to two hours.
Beets, one to five hours.
Turnips, white, forty-five to sixty minutes.
Turnips, yellow, one and a half to two hours.
Parsnips, one or two hours.
Carrots, one or two hours.

SALADS.

SLAW.
Mrs. Sam. Merrill.

Chop the cabbage up fine by itself. Put upon the stove and boil, one pint of vinegar, butter size of an egg, pepper and salt, celery seed. Mix well. Stir, while it boils. Then pour over the cabbage, hot or cold, as preferred.

ONION SLAW.
Mrs. S. E. Wagoner.

Slice very thin two large onions, in one-third cup vinegar. Put in saucepan, boil three minutes, add one heaping teaspoon sugar, one-half teaspoon salt, one teaspoon flour, and pepper to taste.

POTATO SALAD.
Mrs. Burbridge, Crawfordsville.

Boil the potatoes with skins on. Peel them. Chop onions fine, and the potatoes. Season with pepper and salt, and fry with small squares of bacon.

CHICKEN OR TURKEY SALAD.
Mrs. S. L. Goode.

Three joints boned chicken cut into small pieces; pour on this one cup vinegar, two teaspoons mixed mustard, one-half dozen chopped pickles, four stalks celery, five hard boiled eggs. Mix the yolks with three tablespoons of butter into a cream. Add two tablespoons sugar. Mix well all the above ingredients.

POTATO SALAD.
Mrs. S. L. Goode.

One cup vinegar, yolks of three eggs, one-third teaspoon mustard, one-half teaspoon pepper, one teaspoon salt, one and one-half tablespoon sugar, one teaspoon butter, and a medium-sized onion chopped fine. Mix and cook until it thickens; then pour over the potatoes which have been boiled with skins on, peeled, and cut into small squares.

VEAL SALAD.
Mrs. Black.

Substitute boiled veal for chicken—and, as in chicken salad, use celery and hard boiled eggs.

LETTUCE SALAD.

Prepare bunches of lettuce by washing and shredding, and make a dressing of one teaspoon mustard, one tablespoon sugar, yelks of two eggs worked into the mustard and sugar, butter size of an egg, one cup vinegar. Chop the whole, and mix all together.

SALAD DRESSING.

Two hard boiled eggs, one beaten raw egg, one teaspoon each of salt, pepper and made mustard, three teaspoons of salad oil, two teaspoons white sugar, and one-half teacup vinegar.

POTATO SALAD.
Miss Craft.

Boil and peel one-half dozen potatoes; chop them into small bits. One large onion, chopped fine; one-half cup sweet milk or water; one large tablespoonful of butter; one egg, well beaten. Heat milk and butter together, stirring in the beaten egg when it comes to the boiling point; pour this over the potatoes and onions, mixing all together, with salt and pepper to taste. Then pour in a little vinegar to suit taste. This is a nice cold salad; but, if desired warm, it is very nice if fried with some nice drippings of breakfast bacon.

SALADS.

EGG SALAD.
Miss Craft.

Boil eggs until yellows are mealy, then peel and cut into halves, round way; turn yellows out into a dish, mash them fine, mixing in butter, salt, pepper and vinegar, to suit taste. Return this mixture to the white-egg-cups, placing upon dish. This, besides being a good relish with cold meats, is a very pretty dish for table.

LOBSTER SALAD.

Mince the meat of the lobster, and make a dressing of hard boiled eggs, salt, cayenne pepper, mustard, sugar and vinegar. If to be served immediately, add chopped lettuce.

WHITE-FISH OR TROUT SALAD.

To the chopped fish that has been boiled, add either celery, cabbage or lettuce, with salad dressing.

TOMATO SALAD.

Peel and slice the tomatoes. In one raw egg mix hard boiled eggs, salt, pepper, sugar, mustard and vinegar. Smooth the yelks and season them before putting them into the raw egg. Pour this dressing over the tomatoes, and set the dish on ice.

SWEET-BREAD SALAD.
Mrs. Clough.

Wash the sweet-breads and parboil them in hot water. Let them come to a boil. When tender, take off and put in cold water, and let stand until cold; then take them and pull them to pieces. Serve this minced meat with dressing: One heaping teaspoon mustard, one and one-half cups vinegar, one tablespoon sugar and one of melted butter, five eggs beaten separately; and salt to taste. Mix sugar, vinegar, mustard and eggs together.

OYSTER SALAD.
Mrs. Reakirt.

Two-pound can of cove oysters. Beat up four eggs with one cup cream and one cup vinegar, and butter size of an egg. Add one tablespoon each, of mustard, black pepper and sugar; also, a little salt and cayenne pepper. Cook to the consistency of custard. Add rolled crackers. Mix liquor of oysters with this dressing, and pour all upon the oysters. Fresh oysters can be used.

RAW CATSUP.
Mrs. Diehl, Cincinnati.

One peck ripe tomatoes, chopped fine; two horseradish roots, grated fine; one small teacup each, of salt and mustard seed, black and white, mixed; two tablespoons black pepper; two ounces celery seed; one cup onions, chopped fine; one teaspoon ground cloves, one of mace, two of cinnamon; one cup brown sugar, two quarts vinegar. Mix the spices, horseradish, mustard and sugar together. Pour over the ingredients, and mix all thoroughly.

OIL PICKLES.
Mrs. Diehl, Cincinnati.

One hundred cucumbers sliced, one-quarter peck white onions, one quart salt. Put in a press over night; in the morning, add one-quarter pound white mustard seed, the same of ground mustard, of celery seed, black pepper, and one pint of best table oil; then add one gallon of the best cider vinegar.

CURRANT CATSUP.
Mrs. Diehl, Cincinnati.

Three pints currant juice, one-half pound sugar, one tablespoon salt, one teaspoon each of cloves and black pepper, two teaspoons cinnamon, one pint vinegar. Boil sugar and juice ten minutes. Add vinegar at last.

CELERY SALAD.

Cut the celery into bits, and prepare as the tomato salad.

RED PEPPER CATSUP.

Cut up red peppers, and cover with good cider vinegar. Boil slowly, four hours, until perfectly soft. Rub through a sieve. Put up in large-mouthed jars, as the catsup is very thick. It will keep for years.

TOMATO CATSUP.

To one bushel ripe tomatoes add one pint salt. Strain and boil down to one-half. Fifteen minutes before taking off, add two ounces each of cloves, allspice, cayenne pepper, black pepper; and six grated nutmegs. Bottle when cool.

GREEN TOMATO SOY.
Mrs. Mary Kingsbury.

Two gallons tomatoes, twelve good-sized onions. Alternate layers of tomatoes and onions, sprinkling salt on each layer. Slice, in a large stone jar, and let stand over night. Drain off the water; cover with good cider vinegar, and add spice to taste, two tablespoons each of mustard, pepper and cinnamon, one teaspoon cloves, one pint sugar, one tablespoon each, of black and white mustard seed. Mix all together, and stew until tender; stirring often, lest they should scorch. Seal in small glass jars.

CUCUMBER SOY.
Mrs. Mary Kingsbury.

Take large ripe cucumbers; peel, quarter, and take out seeds; grate, and squeeze dry in a cloth; measure the water drained from the cucumbers, and add the amount in vinegar to the dry cucumbers. Season with pepper and salt, a little sugar, and boil about ten minutes. Bottle, and seal as you do catsup.

PICKLES.

MIXED PICKLES.

Mix one-half pound of the best ground mustard and one-half cup of sugar with a little cold vinegar; pour this into a pint of boiling vinegar; let it boil a few minutes and pour over the pickles; slice thin one quart large cucumbers, one pint small cucumbers, one pint onions, one quart green tomatoes, three or four green peppers, and spice to taste. Should cauliflower be added, cut in small pieces. Let all stand in salt one night; drain off and scald in vinegar, and pour over the mixture.

GREEN TOMATO PICKLES.
Mrs. John McClain.

One-half bushel green tomatoes, and six large onions sliced thin. Put over them one cup of salt, and let stand until morning; drain off and boil ten minutes in one quart of vinegar and four quarts water; drain well and boil in four quarts vinegar, with one-fourth pound white mustard seed, three pounds brown sugar, two tablespoons each of red pepper, allspice, cinnamon, cloves and ground mustard.

ARTICHOKE PICKLES.

Rub off the outer skin and lay in salt-water for twenty-four hours; drain and pour over cold, spiced vinegar; add a teaspoonful of horseradish to each can.

BEAN PICKLES

Use the German wax bean, or the Virginia snap bean; string green, young, tender beans; place them in a kettle and boil with salt; drain them; put them in vinegar, with black pepper.

MANGO PICKLES.

Take green muskmelons, cut out a strip lengthwise; take out the seeds; put the melons in brine for twenty-four hours; fill, then, with chopped tomatoes, cabbage, cucumbers, onions and nasturtion seed, all salted separately. Sew the strip cut out on its own melon, and soak in weak cider vinegar all night. In the morning drain off the vinegar and boil it; pour it with one pint of sugar to each gallon of vinegar, boiling hot over the mangoes. Do this several days, and at the last pour over fresh, boiling cider vinegar.

TOMATO PICKLES.
MRS. WILL SIDDALL.

One peck tomatoes, one head cabbage, one dozen onions, six peppers, one gallon vinegar, one-half pound ground mustard, two ounces mustard seed, one ounce celery seed, cloves and cinnamon, one teacup brown sugar. Let it heat one hour.

CHOW-CHOW.

One-half bushel green tomatoes, one dozen onions, one dozen green peppers. Chop all fine; sprinkle over a pint of salt; let it stand one night; drain off the brine; cover with good vinegar; let it cook one hour; drain and pack in a jar; boil in vinegar, mustard, sugar and spices; pour over the mixture.

PICKLED OYSTERS.

One hundred large oysters, one pint vinegar, one dozen blades mace, two dozen each of whole cloves and black peppers, and one large red pepper broken. Put oysters and liquid in kettle; salt to taste; heat slowly, but not to boiling. Take out oysters with perforated skimmer; let them cool, and add the vinegar and spices to the oyster liquor. Boil this liquid, and pour over the oysters. Keep in a dark place.

SLICED GREEN TOMATO PICKLES.

One peck sliced tomatoes. Sprinkle over salt; put in jar, press, and leave over night; next morning put them in colander to drain off the juice. Add to the sliced tomatoes twelve onions sliced, one-half dozen black peppers, one teaspoon red pepper, one ounce mustard, one-half pound mustard seed, one pound brown sugar, one ounce each cloves and allspice. Put in kettle, cover with good vinegar, and boil until tender.

CUCUMBER PICKLES.

One pint of salt to every one hundred cucumbers. Pack in a fresh jar; cover with boiling water; let stand until morning; then wipe the cucumbers, wash out the jar and put layer of pickles, then a layer of sliced onions, cloves, cinnamon, green peppers, black mustard seed, horseradish, and a small lump of alum; pour over boiling water. When the vinegar is boiling, wipe and put in several large grape leaves with the lump of alum. The grape leaves will make the pickles green.

CHOW-CHOW.
Mrs. Reep, Knoxville, Tenn.

Two gallons sliced cabbage, one gallon sliced green tomatoes, twelve sliced onions, one gallon vinegar, one pound brown sugar, one ounce celery seed, one ounce cloves, one gill salt, peppers to suit, one-fourth pound white mustard seed. Boil all together in porcelain or tin.

TO PICKLE CUCUMBERS.
Miss Kittie Lane.

One gallon of vinegar and one cup of salt. Boil and pour over the pickles four or five mornings in succession, and on the last morning put in a small lump of alum. Scald the pickles a minute or two, then put them in a jar, and pour over them fresh vinegar boiled with white ginger root, cinnamon bark and a little cayenne pepper.

MIXED PICKLE.

Mrs. Dickey, Madison.

One-half peck green tomatoes, cut small; one-half peck string beans. Boil alone, till tender. One dozen large cucumbers, cut in inch pieces; one-half dozen green peppers, one-half dozen ochre pods, one-half peck small onions, one head cauliflower. Cover all with salt, and let stand twenty-four hours; rinse with water, and drain well; then add one box ground mustard, three tablespoons each of ground cinnamon and celery seed, one ounce of turmeric. Put in kettle, and cover with vinegar. Seal in glass jars. Scrape two or three horseradish roots, and add sugar if you like.

SWEET-PICKLED TOMATOES.

Mrs. Sam. Merrill.

Slice the tomatoes and sprinkle salt over them; let them drain over night; in the morning throw them into cold water for a few minutes; make a syrup of vinegar, sugar, and spices; scald the tomatoes with this for three mornings, then put them in and let them boil until tender.

CHOPPED PICKLES.

Mrs. Col. Merrill.

One peck green tomatoes, two heads cabbage. Chop and put in salt, separately, over night; also, put one-fourth peck onions in salt; drain the tomatoes, onions and cabbage through a sieve; wash them, rinse them and add one root horseradish, one-half cup each of black and yellow mustard seed, one-half cup unground black pepper, one dozen cloves, and two red peppers, chopped; pour cold vinegar on the mixture.

COLD SLAW.

Cut fine one-half head cabbage; add to it one stalk of celery or one teaspoon celery seed, four hard eggs chopped fine.

COLD TOMATO CATSUP.

One-half peck ripe tomatoes sliced, two horseradish roots grated, one teacup salt, one teacup of sugar, one teacup celery seed, with black and white mustard seed mixed; one large coffeecup sliced onions, two or three red peppers, without seeds, chopped; two or three stalks of celery, two tablespoons black pepper, one teaspoon each of ground cloves, mace, and cinnamon. Mix, put in jars, and pour on boiling vinegar.

CUCUMBER CATSUP.
Mrs. Bently.

Peel a dozen large cucumbers, grate, take out seed and chop fine; add one tablespoon salt; mix and tie up in a thin cloth to drain over night; chop fine six or seven white, medium-sized onions, six or seven green or black peppers, two ounces each of white and black mustard. Mix and put in stone jar and cover with pure cider vinegar; tie cloth over jar, and begin using the catsup two weeks after its making.

TOMATO SLAW.

Peel and seed fresh tomatoes; chop them with celery. Serve with salad dressing.

WALNUT PICKLES.

Rub walnuts well with a coarse towel and lay them for two weeks in a strong brine of salt and water; drain them and cover them in a kettle with fresh water; let them keep hot for twelve hours, but not boil; to one hundred walnuts take one gallon of the best vinegar, one ounce each of pepper and cloves, half an ounce of nutmeg and four ounces of ginger. Let it boil five minutes, pour it out, cover closely, and stand it away to get cold; place the walnuts in jars, and strew over them four ounces of mustard seed, then pour over the spiced vinegar and cover them closely.

WALNUT CATSUP.

When the pickled walnuts are soft, mash through the vinegar, strain and boil thick. Bottle it, put a tablespoon of sweet oil on the top of each bottle, and cork them tightly; seal the corks and it will keep for years.

PICKLED ONIONS.
Mrs. Sappington.

Choose small, white, onions, peel, and throw into boiling salt and water. Place them, when clear, on a seive to dry, then put in more, until all are cooked; add red pepper pods.

CELERY SLAW.

Cut up the celery in inch pieces; make a dressing for it of yelks of three eggs, boiled hard, one small teacup vinegar; one tablespoon salad oil, or butter; one teaspoon mustard; salt and pepper.

HOT SLAW.

Slice the cabbage in long, thin slices; add a little water; thicken cream with flour, and pour over the cabbage when heated; season with pepper and salt; use vinegar, if desired.

CHILI SAUCE.
Mrs. Crane, Chicago.

Twenty-four large, ripe tomatoes, four onions, eight green peppers. Add eight tablespoons brown sugar, four even tablespoons salt, four teaspoons ginger, same of cloves, cinnamon and nutmeg. To the mixture add eight teacups vinegar; stew all together until well cooked.

CUCUMBER AND ONION PICKLE.
Mrs. Carrie Munson.

Equal quantities of large cucumbers and onions; slice and salt them over night, and drain next morning; add a pod or two of green and red peppers, celery seed, cloves, and a small quantity of sugar; press into the jars, pour over hot vinegar, and seal.

PICKLED EGGS.

Boil the eggs hard; remove shell; put in jar of vinegar.

SWEET-PICKLE TOMATO.
Mrs. Rev. Brown, Madison, Ind.

Pick smooth, green tomatoes, slice them and sprinkle lightly with salt; let them stand twenty-four hours in an earthen or stone vessel, then drain off all the water; put them in a kettle with enough vinegar to cover them; add four pounds best brown sugar, one ounce ginger, one-half pound white mustard seed, one ounce pulverized mace. Mix and cook steadily, but slowly, for one hour and a quarter.

CHOPPED PICKLES.
Mrs. Rev. Brown, Madison.

One peck green tomatoes, one dozen large cucumbers, one dozen green peppers, one medium-sized white onion, one head cabbage, one ounce mace, one ounce Jamaica ginger, two ounces cinnamon, five pounds brown sugar, one-half pound white mustard seed, two large tablespoons celery seed, one gallon cider vinegar. After chopping, pour boiling water over the tomatoes and onions; salt lightly and let them lie over night; next morning squeeze gently and put into weak vinegar for twenty-four hours; bring the strong vinegar to a boil, adding the spice, and pour over all in a boiling state.

SLICED CUCUMBER PICKLES.
Mrs. Stearns, Madison, Ind.

One peck cucumbers, peeled and sliced as for table use; let them lie in salt and water twenty-four hours; drain well; cook for two or three minutes in vinegar enough to cover, with the following spices: One cup vinegar, one tablespoon cinnamon, one spoon each of cloves, allspice and white mustard seed. Seal in cans.

PIES.

CREAM PIE.
Mrs Mendenhall.

For the crust take two cups flour, two cups sugar, four eggs, two-thirds of a cup of cold water, one teaspoon baking-powder. Bake in jelly tins—the above being sufficient for six layers or three pies. The cream is to be placed between two crusts; it is made of one pint of milk, two eggs, three tablespoons flour. Let the milk be placed over the fire, and allowed to come to a boil. Add the eggs and flour, well beaten together; and while boiling, add salt and flavoring.

CREAM PIE.
Miss Jessie Wiley.

Beat thoroughly together with the white of one egg, one-half teacup sugar and tablespoonful of flour; then add one teacup of milk. Bake with pastry crust, and grate nutmeg on top.

VINEGAR PIE.
Miss Jessie Wiley.

One egg, one heaping spoon flour, one teacup sugar; beat all well together, and add one tablespoon sharp vinegar, one cup cold water; flavor with nutmeg.

GREEN APPLE PIE.
Mrs. Reynolds.

Use sliced, sour apples, raw; season with butter, sugar and cinnamon.

VINEGAR PIE.
Mrs. L. Henderson, Greenwood.

One cup sugar, one egg, one cup water, one tablespoon flour, one teaspoon lemon, one tablespoon vinegar.

TOMATO PIE.
Mrs. Kellog.

Select large ripe tomatoes; scald off the peeling; slice one layer to each pie. Add one-half cup sugar, one teaspoon butter. Flavor with nutmeg and cinnamon, dust in a little flour, and cover with a rich paste.

CREAM APPLE PIE.
Mrs. Kellog.

Line pie plate with puff paste; drop in stewed green apples in tablespoonfuls, leaving it rough and uneven; sift in a little flour, one-half teacup sugar and fill with rich cream.

LEMON PIE.
Mrs. Sam. Merrill.

To the juice and grated rind of two large lemons, add one tablespoon melted butter, yelks of six eggs, whites of three eggs, and twelve tablespoons sugar.

CREAM PIE.
Mrs. J. M. Binford.

The yelk of one egg; two tablespoons sugar, one tablespoon melted butter, one heaping tablespoon corn starch or flour; milk to fill pie dish. Flavor with lemon, and bake. Beat the white of egg, and spread over the pie; return to oven, and brown.

COCOA-NUT PIE.
Mrs. Noah Clark.

Three eggs, one glass of cocoa-nut, one pint of milk. Beat the eggs separately, and make as for custard pie, adding the cocoa-nut.

LEMON PIE.
Mrs. E. Carnes, Greenwood.

One grated lemon, two cups rich milk, one cup sugar, two spoons butter, and four eggs beaten separately. Enough for two pies.

CHESS PIE.
Mrs. S. L. Goode.

Two cups sugar, one-half cup butter, eight eggs, leaving out the whites of five for frosting, one tablespoon corn starch in one cup milk; lemon flavoring. Bake in under crust; then ice, and brown slightly.

LEMON PIE.
Mrs. Dr. McWhorter, Calhoun, Tenn.

One cup sugar, one-half cup sweet cream, two small lemons, two eggs. If you have no cream, use sweet milk, and then add one tablespoon melted butter. Beat the yelks of the eggs very light, add the sugar, and beat again; then add the juice of both lemons, and the grated rind of one. Line pie-pan with crust; add the cream to the mixture, just before putting into the oven. Bake until the custard is firm; draw to the front of the oven, and spread evenly over the top a meringue of the whites of the two eggs, beaten stiff, with two tablespoons sugar; return to the oven until it sets. To be eaten cold.

LEMON PIE.
Mrs. Rodman.

For one pie: One lemon, rind grated and juice squeezed; one cup sugar, one cup sweet milk, two eggs, butter size of a walnut, two tablespoons corn starch. Save the whites of the two eggs to beat with the tablespoon of sugar. After baking the pie, spread over this frosting and put in the oven to brown lightly.

MOCK MINCE PIE.
Mrs. M. A. E. Eckert.

One cup bread crumbs, two cups cold water, two cups molasses, one cup brown sugar, one cup vinegar, one cup melted butter, one cup chopped raisins, one egg beaten light and stirred in at the last; add spices. Rolled cracker may be substituted for the bread crumbs.

DRIED APPLE PIE.
Mrs. F. Rubush.

Cook the apples and mash fine; flavor with lemon peel; sweeten according to the quality of the apples and the richness of the sauce; make neither too thick nor too thin.

VINEGAR PIE.
Mrs. Craig.

One pint of water, one tablespoon each of butter and vinegar. In one-fourth of the pint of water beat flour sufficient to make a thick starch; stir and cook all together; sweeten and flavor to taste; let cool and fill the pie-pans.

CREAM PIE.
Mrs. Craig.

Rub fine into crumbs one-half slice of bread, leaving out the crust; add the yelk of one egg, three-fourths of a pint of new milk, one tablespoon butter. Sweeten to taste; flavor with nutmeg, and bake.

DRIED APPLE PIE.
Mrs. F. Rubush.

Cook the apples, after soaking, and cook cranberries until tender; mash the apples and mix with them the cooked cranberries, half and half; sweeten to taste; put on upper crust.

BLACKBERRY PIE.
Mrs. Reynolds.

Line a deep pie-dish with paste; fill half full of blackberries; add one-half teacup sugar, one tablespoon butter, and if berries are very juicy, sprinkle in a little flour; add more sugar and berries; cover with a good crust and bake slowly

PUMPKIN PIE.
Mrs. Reynolds.

Two quarts pumpkin, strained; one quart milk, three eggs, spice and sugar to taste.

PLUM PIE.
Mrs. Reynolds.

Let the plums simmer in a little sugar and water until tender; take them out, add plenty of sugar to the juice, and boil until it begins to thicken; turn it over the plums and set aside to cool; when cold line pie-pans or plates with a rich paste, fill, cover, and bake half an hour.

LEMON PIE.
Miss Anna Allisson.

For two pies: Three eggs, one cup sugar, one tablespoon water, three or four teaspoons flour, grate and squeeze two small lemons, spread the whites of eggs beaten to a froth and sweetened to taste on the top, and return to oven to brown slightly.

COCOANUT PIE.

One coffeecup milk, two eggs, one grated cocoanut, one-half teacup sugar. Flavor with lemon.

TENNESSEE SWEET POTATO PIE.
Mr. Erwin.

Parboil, skin, and slice crosswise, firm sweet potatoes. Line a dish with pastry; put in a layer of sweet potatoes, sprinkled thick with sugar; scatter a few whole cloves upon it, and cover with more slices; fill the dish in this way. Add melted butter, pour in a little water, and cover with crust. This pie is best as a cobbler, with jelly or preserves.

LEMON PIE.
Mrs. M. A. E. Eckert.

Line the pie-pan with good, puff paste; grate outside peel over it; peel all the white part off; slice the lemon very thin, and put in layers over the grated peeling; sprinkle one cup sugar and one teaspoon flour over the slices; almost fill the pan with water and cover with crust.

AUNT CHARLOTTE PIES.
Mrs. Black.

Three pints milk, thickened with flour, when boiling, as thick as starch—the flour wet with cold milk. Beat eight eggs separately; add eight tablespoons of sugar to the yelks. Melt three-fourths of a pound of butter in the boiling milk. Mix all into a batter. Stir in the beaten whites, flavor with lemon and nutmeg. Bake until brown. This makes five pies, with no upper crust.

CUSTARD PIE.
Mrs. Bugbee.

One pint milk, three eggs, three tablespoons white sugar, and a pinch of salt. Beat the eggs and sugar thoroughly, and put them into the milk. The pies may be filled immediately, and set into the oven.

CHESS PIE.
Miss Georgie Howell.

Two cups white sugar, one small cup butter, one cup sweet milk, five eggs, one teaspoon lemon or vanilla, one tablespoon flour; grate nutmeg on the crust. This will make two pies.

JELLY PIE.
Mrs. Springer.

One cup jelly, one cup butter, one cup sugar, five eggs, one-half cup milk.

PUMPKIN PIE.
Mrs. Lowe.

One egg for each pie, three tablespoons pumpkin, two tablespoons sugar, one coffeecup milk.

PUMPKIN PIE.
Mrs. Yonce, Franklin.

Stew pumpkin all day; then strain through the colander. Put in butter size of an egg for each pie, two eggs, and one-half pint cream or milk. Season with cinnamon.

APPLE CUSTARD PIE.
Mrs. Bugbee.
Put apple sauce through the colander. Let there be three eggs for each pie, one-third of a cup of butter, and same of sugar, for each pie. A frosting of the whites of the eggs and sugar improves the appearance of the pies. Set them in the oven to brown.

LEMON CUSTARD PIE.
Mrs. Hereth.
Grated rind of one lemon, one egg (omitting the white), one-half cup sugar, one tablespoon flour. Beat all together and then add one cup milk; bake in a rich crust.

LEMON PIE.
Miss Fannie Bugbee.
To the beaten whites of the egg add one tablespoon pulverized white sugar, and after baking, grate and squeeze the juice of one lemon; place upon the stove to thicken a very little; one cup of water, one cup of sugar, two teaspoons corn-starch, the juice and grated peel of the lemon, and four eggs, reserving the whites of two of the eggs for frosting. Line the pie-pan with pastry, and bake; then fill with the mixture; beat the reserved whites to a stiff froth; spread on the top of the pie that has baked, and put in the oven to brown lightly.

LAYER PIE.
Mrs. Sappington, Madison.
Make a rich pastry, and bake as thin as possible in jelly-pans; boil until thick one quart of milk, one cup sugar, four tablespoonfulls corn-starch. When cold, spread; if not wanted the day made, do not spread; flavor to taste.

JAM PIE.
Mrs. Springer.
One cup jam, such as blackberry or raspberry; two eggs, one cup sugar, one of butter. Excellent.

LEMON PIE.
Mrs. Craig.

Juice and pulp of one lemon, one egg, four tablespoons sugar, one tablespoon butter. Take the whites of two eggs, beaten to a froth, and add one teaspoon sugar, and return to the quick oven.

MINCE PIE.
Mrs. C. O. Page, Madison.

Two pounds suet, two pounds apples, two pounds raisins, two pounds currants, two pounds sugar, three pounds beef, one pound citron, one ounce salt, one-half ounce allspice, one-half ounce cloves, one-half ounce cinnamon, two quarts sweet cider.

LEMON PIE.

Dissolve one tablespoon corn-starch in cold water, and then stir it into one cup boiling water; cream or rub one tablespoonful of butter with one cup of sugar, and pour over the hot corn-starch; when quite cool, add one lemon and one beaten egg; take inner rind and mince small; bake with one crust.

LEMON PIE.
Mrs. Kate Haines, Connersville.

Add to the grated rind and juice of one lemon, three eggs, saving the whites of two; add to the lemon and eggs, one and one-half cups sugar, two tablespoons flour and one teaspoon butter; pour on this two teacups hot water, and boil until it thickens; make crust for two pies, and bake; then pour in the custard and cover with the whites of the two eggs.

MOCK MINCE PIE.
Mrs. Eckert.

One teacup bread crumbs, two cups each of cold water and molasses, one cup of brown sugar; one cup each, of vinegar, melted butter, and chopped raisins.

STRAWBERRY SHORTCAKE.
Mrs. Black.

Bake in jelly cake pans a baking-powder biscuit dough. Split open, and cover both parts with butter and ripe strawberries; put one section upon the other, and cover the top with white sugar. Eat with cream.

POTATO CUSTARD.
Mrs. Haughey.

Six potatoes; one cup each, of butter and sugar; five eggs and one nutmeg. Bake in crust.

GERMAN PUFFS.
Mrs. Haughey.

One quart milk, one-half pound flour; eight eggs, beaten separately. Prepare boiled sauce.

LEMON CUSTARD PIE.
Mrs. Kring.

One coffeecup sugar; five eggs, leaving out whites of two, two tablespoons of flour, one coffeecup hot water. Beat yelks of eggs with the flour. Add two grated lemons. This makes two pies. Beat together the whites of the two eggs with three tablespoons of sugar. Spread over the top, and set in oven a moment, but not to brown. The best lemon pie that can be made.

PUDDINGS.

CITRON PUDDING.
Mrs. Basore, Broadway, Virginia.

Yelks of sixteen eggs, three-fourths pound butter, one pound white sugar, twelve drops essence of lemon; a layer of chipped citron and pudding alternately. A choice recipe.

LEMON PUDDING.
Mrs. Basore, Broadway, Virginia.

One-half pound sugar, one-half pound butter, yelks of eight eggs, a little nutmeg, and two fresh lemons.

FIG PUDDING.
Mrs. Binford.

One pint bread crumbs, one cup suet, one cup brown sugar, two eggs, one-half pound figs. Wash the figs in warm water; dry in a cloth; chop the suet and figs together; add the other ingredients, also one nutmeg grated. Boil three hours and serve with hard sauce.

LEMON PUDDING.
Mrs. S. A. Newton, Cincinnati, Ohio.

One quart milk, two cups bread crumbs, four eggs, one-half cup butter, one cup white sugar, one large lemon rind grated. Soak the bread in the milk, add the beaten yelks with the butter and sugar rubbed to a cream; bake in a quick oven; whites beaten and put on the top, return to the oven to brown.

CAKE PUDDING.
Mrs. Reynolds.

Layers of raisins and layers of cakes, alternate; put in the dish sufficient milk to moisten the cakes; steam twenty minutes, and serve with sauce.

A QUICK PUDDING.
Mrs S. A. Newton, Cincinnati, Ohio.

Split a few crackers, lay the surface over with raisins, and place the halves together; tie them closely in a cloth and boil them fifteen minutes in milk and water. Eat with a rich sauce.

CABINET PUDDING.

Butter a mold, cover the bottom with raisins and citron, next a layer of cake, and so alternate; mix in a bowl three tablespoons sugar and the yelks of three eggs and put them in a pint of boiling milk; pour over the cake and fruit, and put into the oven to bake. Serve with sauce.

COCOANUT PUDDING.
Mrs. Mendenhall.

Grate one cocoanut fine; add to it four ounces of melted butter, four ounces loaf-sugar, four eggs, and the rind and juice of one lemon; line the dish with a rich paste; fill with the mixture. Bake, and serve cold.

FRENCH PUDDING.
Miss Dods.

Five ounces bread crumbs, three ounces sugar, three ounces raisins, two ounces almonds, two ounces citron, one-half pint milk, three eggs, teaspoon lemon juice. Pour into a greased mold and steam for an hour and twenty minutes.

RICE DESSERT.

One quart sweet milk, two-thirds cup rice, a little salt. Put this in teacups; set in a steamer over a kettle of boiling water. Let it cook until the rice is like jelly. When cold, turn out of the cup. Eat with cream or sauce. A few raisins in each cup is an addition.

BAKED ROLL PUDDING.
Mrs. Mary E. Lowe.

One quart flour, one tablespoon baking-powder, one teaspoon salt, two tablespoons lard and sweet milk, sufficient to make a dough, as for baking-powder biscuit. Rub the baking-powder through the flour; add salt and lard, lastly the milk, taking care not to knead too much. Roll out quickly on a bread-board; spread well with fruit of any kind. Roll up like a jelly cake roll; spread the top over well with butter first, then with a layer of sugar. Pour in the pan a half pint of water, and bake slowly for two hours. Serve when a little warm, with cream, or prepared sauce as follows: One tablespoon flour, smoothed with a little cold water; one pint of boiling water, one tablespoon of butter, one teacup sugar, one tablespoon vinegar, and a very little salt. Let it boil a few minutes, and flavor to taste.

FARMER'S APPLE PUDDING.
Miss Lida Wheat.

If apples are juicy, they will require very little water to stew them. Add to one pound of the mashed apple when hot, one-fourth pound butter and sugar to taste. Beat four eggs, and stir in when the apple is cold. Butter the bottom and sides of a deep pudding dish, strew it thickly with bread crumbs, put in the mixture, and strew bread crumbs over the top. When baked, sift sugar over.

CHARLOTTE RUSSE.
Mrs. Reynolds.

Dissolve one ounce of gelatine in a little tepid water; beat one egg in one cup of milk; add two tablespoons sugar; flavor with vanilla; pour it over the gelatine; let it stand until cold; whip one quart sweet cream, taking off the froth as it rises, into a bowl; then stir in the mixture; line pans with small sponge cakes, or lady-fingers; pour over the cakes this mixture, and set the pans on ice.

CREAM WHIPS.
Mrs. Reynolds.

Whites of eight eggs, beaten to a stiff froth; one pint of rich, sweet cream. Sweeten and flavor the cream to taste; beat it enough to dissolve the sugar. Stir in the froth quickly. Let it stand until cold. Serve in glasses, with tablespoonful of jelly at the bottom of each glass.

STEAMED ROLY-POLY.

Roll biscuit dough one-quarter of an inch thick; spread it with fruit, leaving an inch each end uncovered. Roll it tight; sew it in a cloth, giving room to swell. Boil, or steam it one hour. Sponge cake, baked in sheets, makes a good roly-poly pudding. Any kind of sauce.

APPLE MERINGUE.

Boil tart apples; mash fine and sweeten. To one pint add the beaten whites of three eggs. Flavor with rind and juice of a lemon. Put it in a pudding dish, and spread over it the beaten white of the eggs, sweetened.

CHARLESTON PUDDING.
Mrs. J. E. Springer.

One cup and a half sugar, one-half cup butter, one-half cup milk, three eggs, two cups flour, in which is sifted two teaspoons baking-powder.

SAUCE.

One pint water, six tablespoons sugar, one large spoon butter. Bring to a boil; add one teaspoon corn-starch; flavor.

COTTAGE PUDDING.
Mrs. J. E. Springer.

One-half teacup sugar, one-half small teacup butter, one egg, one pint flour, two teaspoons baking-powder. To be eaten with sauce.

SLICED-BREAD PUDDING.
Mrs Reynolds.

Slice bread in thin slices; spread with butter and lay in pudding dish; pour over them milk and eggs to form a custard; two eggs to one pint of milk. Season with spice if you prefer, and keep in oven until custard is formed.

TAPIOCA PUDDING.

Soak three tablespoons tapioca in cold water; when perfectly tender, cook it in one quart of milk, to which add the yelks of three eggs, one cup sugar; flavor with vanilla; pour one-half into a dish, and upon that the whites beaten to a froth, and over this the other half.

TAPIOCA PUDDING.

One quart tapioca soaked over night in one quart water; fill pudding dish with the halves of apples; mix large cup of sugar with the tapioca; pour it over the apples and bake one hour. Eat with cream.

SNOW PUDDING.

Dissolve one cup gelatine in a pint of boiling water; add two cups sugar, juice two lemons; strain, and when cold add the whites of two eggs beaten to a stiff froth. Beat this mixture thoroughly. Make a custard of the yelks of two eggs, one whole egg, and one pint of milk to serve with the snow pudding.

APPLE PUDDING.
Mrs. Springer.

Peel and slice apples in a pan; cook them in the oven with very little water, and afterwards sweeten them; while hot pour over a batter made of one egg, one tablespoon sugar, a piece of butter size of an egg, one cup of milk, and flour to make like cake-batter; add one teaspoon baking-powder; flavor; eat with cream or sauce.

APPLE PUDDING.

A layer of sliced apples in the dish; sprinkle them with cinnamon, nutmeg and sugar; then add a layer of bread crumbs, with pieces of butter; next a layer of apples, and so fill the dish, letting the bread crumbs be on the top. Eat with sauce.

PIEPLANT PUDDING.
Miss Georgie Howell.

Cut pieplant into inch-long pieces; fill a pudding dish with alternate layers of the pieplant and bread crumbs, putting the bread crumbs, with sugar and butter, on the bottom; let there be one pound of sugar to one pound of pieplant; serve with boiled custard. This pudding is best when eaten neither hot nor cold, but only warm.

CRACKER PUDDING.
Mrs. Lowe.

One-half pound of crackers, crumbled fine, or rolled as for soup; cover them with a sauce of one pint boiling water, one tablespoon flour smoothed with cold water, one tablespoon butter and sugar to make very sweet. Flavor with nutmeg. Let the dish be covered tight, after pouring the sauce over the crackers.

CRACKER PUDDING.
Mrs. Paul Hereth.

Powder crackers finely; add one-half nutmeg, one-half cup sugar and one-half cup butter. Beat eight eggs to a stiff froth, and mix with one quart milk. Pour over the crackers, to soften them before baking.

BROWN PUDDING.
Mrs. S. H. Crane, Chicago.

One-half cup of melted butter, one cup of molasses, one teaspoon soda, one cup cold water, three cups flour; add raisins or currants. Steam three hours. Serve with a rich sauce.

CHOCOLATE PUDDING.
Mrs. S. H. Crane, Chicago.

Five tablespoons grated chocolate, ten tablespoons grated bread or crackers, one quart milk with bread scalded in it. When partly cold, stir in the chocolate, one cup of sugar, and the yelks of five eggs. Bake about half an hour. Beat the whites of the eggs, add one small cup of sugar. Cover the top of the pudding with this stiff froth, and set it in the oven to brown. Serve cold.

COCOANUT PUDDING.
Mrs. S. H. Crane, Chicago.

Soak over night, or for two or three hours, four tablespoons of tapioca. Put a pan with one quart of milk into a pan of boiling water, until the milk boils; then add the tapioca. Let it boil five minutes. Beat together the yelks of four eggs, one cup of sugar, five tablespoons of grated cocoanut, juice of one lemon; add this to the milk and tapioca. Pour into a dish, and bake half an hour. Frost the pudding with the whites of the eggs and three tablespoons of sugar. Over this sprinkle cocoanut thickly.

PENNSYLVANIA PUDDING.
Mrs. S. H. Crane, Chicago.

One small cup gelatine into a quart of milk; let it come to a boil. Beat the yelks of four eggs and one cup of sugar together; then pour the hot milk over them, stirring all the time. Put on the stove until of the consistency of custard; take off, and stir in the whites beaten to a stiff froth. Flavor with vanilla, and serve it cold with cream.

SUET PUDDING.
Mrs. Jas. Chapin.

One quart bread crumbs, soaked; two eggs, one cup of suet, one cup currants, one pint flour. Boil, or steam one hour and a half. Eat with sauce.

Carpet Department.

We have the MOST COMPLETE LINE OF CARPETS, in all their qualities, that we have ever carried, consisting of

Moquettes, Tapestry Brussels,
Velvets, 3-Plys and
Body Brussels, Ingrains.
BORDERS TO MATCH.

Drapery Department.

We pride ourselves on the styles and qualities of our Laces. We always have on hand all the Novelties in

Appliquet, Tambour, Antique, Guipare and Nottingham Laces.

Wall Papers and Decorations

A SPECIALTY.

OUR RUG DEPARTMENT

IS REPLETE IN ALL THE NOVELTIES.

COME AND SEE US. NO TROUBLE TO SHOW GOODS.

W. H. ROLL,

Nos. 30, 32 & 34 S. Illinois Street,
INDIANAPOLIS, IND.

EDMUND B. NOEL.   WOOD NOEL.

NOEL BROS.,
JOBBERS OF
Gibson & Co's Flour,
ALSO,
Grain, Feed, Meal, Cracked Wheat,
Oat Meal, Hominy, etc.

69 North Illinois St.,   **INDIANAPOLIS, IND.**

1865.   1882.

GROCERIES,
Teas, Coffee, Spices, etc.

H. N. GOE'S

Long experience in the Grocery Business enables him to offer, at all times, as good an assortment of the very best goods as can be found in the city. He is now offering the best brands of CANNED GOODS, by the case or dozen, at low figures. CALL FOR PRICES!

Feed of all kinds, Poultry, Fruits, Vegetables
ALWAYS IN STOCK.

TELEPHONE CONNECTION.

2 and 4 Central Ave. and 527 N. Illinois St.,

INDIANAPOLIS, IND.

BAMBERGER,
"THE HATTER"

Is prepared the year round with all the latest styles in

Hats, Caps and Furs

FOR MEN AND BOYS.

Don't Forget the Old Reliable Stand,

16 EAST WASHINGTON STREET.

BROWNING & SLOAN,
→DRUGGISTS←

AND DEALERS IN

FINE FLAVORING EXTRACTS,

PURE GROUND AND UNGROUND SPICES,

Fine, Perfumery and Toilet Articles; Labin's, Atkinson's, Colgate, Lundberg and Recksecker's Fine Extracts; Genuine Imported Farina and German Cologne; Florida and Lavender Waters; Fine Toilet Soaps and Sponges; Tooth, Hair, Cloth and Nail Brushes; Bath Towels and Brushes; Fine Cosmetics, Combs, Dressing Cases, Cologne Sets, Fine Toilet Powders, and all articles wanted for the toilet at the lowest figures.

APOTHECARIES' HALL,

7 & 9 E. Washington St.,   INDIANAPOLIS, IND.

FURNAS'

STANDARD

ICE CREAM

Grows in popularity, and it is a satisfaction to the proprietor to know that an honest effort to produce a strictly first-class article has been fully appreciated.

No effort will be spared to procure the very best material, and to raise, if possible, the standard of quality.

TRY OUR BUTTER,

WHICH WE MAKE DAILY.

—

R. W. FURNAS,

54 Massachusetts Avenue.

SUET PUDDING.
Miss Sue Bugbee.

One cup molasses, one cup sweet milk, one cup suet chopped fine, three and one-half cups flour, one cup raisins, one teaspoon soda. cinnamon, cloves and allspice, Steam three hours; eat with sauce.

SUET CORN MEAL PUDDING.

Boil one quart milk; mix with it one and one-half cups corn meal, one-half cup suet, two eggs, one cup molasses, and one teacup raisins. Add cinnamon or nutmeg.

SUET PUDDING.
Miss. Wood.

One cup suet chopped fine, two cups raisins, one cup milk, one cup currants, one cup molasses, three cups flour, one teaspoon soda dissolved in the molasses. Beat all together and boil three hours. Eat with sauce.

CORN MEAL PUDDING.
Miss J. M. Crane, Madison.

One quart milk; let it come to a boil, and then stir in two yelks of eggs, one cup of sugar, three heaping tablespoons corn meal. When it begins to thicken, turn into a pan and stir through it whites of the eggs, beaten stiff; flavor and put in oven to brown. Eat warm with cream.

BAKED INDIAN PUDDING.
Mrs. Bugbee.

Boil one quart of milk; stir in one cup of corn meal, one-half cup flour, also two-thirds of a cup molasses; butter size of an egg; bake slowly five hours.

ENGLISH STEAMED PUDDING.
Mrs. Lowe.

One teacup chopped suet, one cup sugar, four eggs, five cups flour, one teaspoon soda, one pound raisins, sour milk to make stiff batter. Steam three or four hours.

PLUM PUDDING.
Mrs. Hereth.

One cup sugar, one cup molasses, one cup suet chopped fine, one cup sweet milk, flour to make stiff batter; add one cup dredged raisins, one teaspoon each of cinnamon, allspice and cloves; sift in the flour two teaspoons baking-powder, and a little salt; steam three hours. Serve with sauce.

RICE PUDDING.

One-half cup uncooked rice, one quart milk one tablespoon butter, little salt. Sweeten to taste. One cup of raisins improves rice pudding. Bake well.

BATTER PUDDING.
Mrs. Pogue, Madison.

One egg, one cup sugar, one cup milk, two cups flour, one teaspoon baking-powder, one cup currants or raisins; cinnamon or nutmeg. Steam one and one-half hours.

BLACKBERRY SLUMP.
Mrs. Black.

Fill a tin pan half full of the hot-stewed fruit; cover it with baking-powder biscuit dough; cover tightly with tin lid, if baked on the stove; if it is in the stove, or in a covered kettle of boiling water, no lid is needed. Eat with a rich sauce.

CORN-STACH PUDDING.
Mrs. Springer.

One quart milk, three eggs, one tablespoon sugar. When the milk is almost boiling, rub two tablespoons corn starch in cold milk, and put it with the yelks of three eggs and one tablespoon sugar; then add to the milk. and boil all together. Beat the whites of the eggs with a little sugar, and, as you take the pudding off the stove, beat into it the whites.

CORN-STARCH PUDDING.

Make as above, excepting it should get almost cold; spread jelly almost over it, and then the beaten whites of the eggs.

COTTAGE PUDDING.
Miss Jessie Wiley.

One cup sugar, one-half cup butter, one egg, one cup sweet milk, one teaspoon soda dissolved in milk, two teaspoons cream tartar in the flour, three cups flour, one-half teaspoon extract lemon. Sprinkle a little sugar over the top, just before putting into the oven. Bake in a small bread pan, and when done, cut in squares. Serve with sauce made of two tablespoons butter, cup sugar, tablespoon flour wet with a little cold water and stirred until like cream. Add one pint boiling water. Let boil two or three minutes, stirring all the time. After taking from the fire, add one-half teaspoon of extract lemon or nutmeg. What is left of the pudding may be served cold for tea.

CREAM PUDDDING.
Miss Jessie Wiley.

Stir together one pint cream, three ounces sugar, yelks of three eggs, and a little grated nutmeg; add the well beaten whites, stirring lightly. Pour into a buttered pie-pan, in which has been sprinkled crumbs of stale bread to about the thickness of an ordinary pie-crust. Sprinkle over the top a layer of bread crumbs.

GELATINE PUDDING.

Two tablespoons gelatine; pour over it one pint boiling water, and sweeten to taste; prepare this at night, and set in a cold place; in the morning make a custard of one pint milk, sugar, and the yelks of three eggs; beat the whites to a stiff froth, and just before serving cut the jelly into small squares; pour over the squares the whites of the eggs, and then the custard. It is well to let the jelly form in the dish from which it is served.

ORANGE SOUFFLE.
Miss Jessie Wiley.

Peel and slice six oranges. Put into a high glass dish a layer of orange, then one of sugar, and so alternate until all the orange is used. Let stand two hours. Make a soft boiled custard of the yelks of three eggs, one pint milk, sufficient sugar, with a grating of orange peel for flavor; pour over the oranges, when cool. Beat the whites of the eggs to a stiff froth, stir in sugar, and pour over the pudding.

ORANGE PUDDING.
Mrs. S. M. Sappington, Madison.

Grate rind and squeeze juice of two dark oranges. Beat together one-half cup sugar, one heaping tablespoon butter, and the yelks of three eggs. Stir into the orange. Put into a buttered dish, after stirring in the beaten whites of the eggs. Bake half an hour, and, when cool, grate white sugar over. Eat cold.

SNOW PUDDING.

One cup gelatine; pour three and one-half cups water over it. Prepare it at night, and next morning add two cups sugar and juice of two lemons. Strain, and set in a cool place until it begins to jelly. Add the whites of three eggs, well beaten. Stir in well, and pour into a mold.

QUEEN OF PUDDINGS.
Mrs. Enos.

One pint of bread crumbs, one quart of milk, one cup of sugar, yelks of four eggs, beaten, grated rind of a lemon, and a piece of butter the size of an egg. Bake until done, but not watery. Whip the whites of the egg stiff, and add one teacup of sugar, in which has been stirred the juice of the lemon. Spread over the pudding a layer of jelly, or any other sweet meats, and cover with the whites of the eggs. Replace in the oven, and brown slightly.

ARROW-ROOT PUDDING.

Boil one quart of milk and mix arrow-root in it until it is a thick batter; add six eggs, one-half pound butter, and one-half pound sugar, one-half nutmeg, and a little grated lemon peel. When done, sift sugar over the top.

BUTTER ROLL.
Mrs. Sappington.

Make baking-powder biscuit dough; put in plenty of shortening; roll thin; have ready one and one-half teacups sugar, one cup butter highly flavored with nutmeg; spread this mixture over the dough, and roll up; bake the roll in a pan with two teacups of water; there is then sauce enough. This is a royal pudding.

BIRD'S-NEST SAGO PUDDING.
Mrs. Enos.

Soak one-half pint of sago in three pints of water. Pare and core ten or twelve apples; fill the centers of the apples with the sago, and put them, without piling one over another, in a pudding dish, so that the sago will just cover them. Bake until the apples are soft. Eat with sauce.— Sauce: One teacup sugar, one-half teacup butter, one-half cup water, and one teaspoon flour; boil and flavor.

BIRD'S-NEST PUDDING
Mrs. Hereth.

Make a batter as for batter cakes. Pare apples and core them, putting pieces of apple in teacups, filling with the egg batter two-thirds of the cups, giving space for rising. Steam an hour and a half. Eat with either hard or liquid sauce.

STRAWBERRY PUDDING.
Mrs. S. H. Crane, Chicago.

Cover the Queen of Puddings with canned strawberries or jelly. Add the well beaten whites, and set in the oven to brown. Serve cold, with cream.

STEAMED PUDDING.
Mrs. R. G. Graydon, Southport.

One cup of molasses, one cup of sugar, one cup suet or butter, one cup sweet milk, one teaspoon soda, one cup raisins, one cup currants, spice to taste; add flour until very stiff. Steam three hours, and try it with a straw. Eat with liquid sauce. Steam, whenever desired for the table, as it will keep for weeks.

BANANA CREAM.
Mrs. Mary J. Downey, Irvington.

Dissolve one-half box gelatine in one-half teacup cold water. Put one and one-half cups new milk over the fire, after sweetening to taste. When boiling, pour into it the gelatine. Stir until the gelatine is thoroughly dissolved; then boil ten minutes, and when cold, but not stiff, stir in six bananas, sliced with a silver knife. Mix well, and set away on ice. One hour before using, take a pint of rich cream, sweeten to taste, flavor with vanilla, and whip well. Put the mixture first made into a glass dish, and pour over it the whipped cream.

PUDDING.
Mrs. Baggs.

One quart milk, two tablepoons corn starch, and the yelks of two eggs; boil all together, as for custard. Take one heaping cup brown sugar, and place in skillet dry, over fire. Stir until dissolved into liquid. Stir in the above custard. Flavor with vanilla. Put into pan and bake. Then meringue with the white of the eggs and four tablespoons sugar. Serve cold, with sweet cream.

LEMON PUDDING.
Mrs. Dr. Wiley.

Take the juice and grated rind of one lemon, one cup sugar, yelks of two eggs, three full tablespoons flour, pinch of salt, one pint rich milk. Mix the flour and part of the milk to a smooth paste. Add the juice and rind of the lemon, the cup of sugar, well beaten yelks, and remainder of the milk. Line a plate with puff paste, one-fourth of an inch thick; pour in the custard, and bake in a quick oven. Beat the whites of two eggs to a stiff froth, and add two tablespoons sugar. Spread over the top, and return to oven to brown. Serve with very cold cream. Sufficient for six persons.

SWEET POTATO PUDDING.
Mrs. Josephine Nichols.

Boil one pound sweet potatoes tender; rub them while hot through a colander; add six eggs well beaten, three-quarters pound sugar, one-half pound butter, a little grated nutmeg and lemon peel; sprinkle the tops with sugar and bits of citron.

HEN'S-NEST PUDDING.
Mrs. Josephine Nichols.

Make a hole in the end of an egg and empty it, leaving shell to be filled with blanc-mange; when stiff and cold take off the shell. A number of these eggs should be placed in a nest made of lemon peel cut into small pieces and preserved in sugar. Fill a dish part full of jelly; place the lemon straws on the jelly, and the eggs on the nest.

CRANBERRY PUDDING.
Mrs. Baggs.

One pint cranberries stirred into a batter a little thicker than batter pudding. Boil and eat with sauce.

GELATINE BLANC-MANGE.
Mrs. Louise Tousey.

Soak one teaspoon gelatine in one and a half pints of milk for one hour; put it over boiling water, or in a vessel set in another of boiling water; when it comes to a boil add the beaten yelks of three eggs with four tablespoons of sugar; when cooling add beaten whites of the eggs; flavor with vanilla, cool in a mold and serve with sugar and cream.

SAGO PUDDING, WITH APPLES.

One tablespoon sago to one large apple; mix sago with warm water; pour boiling water over it; cook to thickness of starch; slice the apples and mix the sago with them; add sugar and bake. Eat with sugar and cream.

SAGO PUDDING.
Mrs. Josephine Nichols.

One and one-half pints new milk, four spoons sago nicely washed and picked, lemon peel, cinnamon, nutmeg. Sweeten and add four eggs; bake in a dish lined with pastry.

ANGEL FOOD.
Mrs. Springer.

Dissolve one and one-half boxes of gelatine in one quart milk; add the well-beaten yelks of three eggs, one cup sugar, and the juice of one lemon; let all come to a boil; take from the stove, and when nearly cold, stir in the whites of the eggs, beaten stiff, and turn in a mold to cool.

CUSTARD PUDDING.
Mrs. Josephine Nichols.

Five eggs to one quart of milk and a coffeecup of sugar. To make boiled custard, first heat the milk; then mix the eggs in a little cold milk; add the sugar and eggs to the hot milk; stir while boiling. To make baked custard, mix all together cold, and put in oven to bake.

BLANC-MANGE.
Mrs. J. R. Nichols.

Mix one tablespoon sea-moss farina with a little cold milk; add one quart milk, and a half teacup powdered sugar and two beaten eggs; a little salt; heat slowly; boil fifteen minutes, stirring; when cooling, flavor and pour into molds.

SIMPLE TAPIOCA PUDDING.
Mrs. Nichols.

Dissolve one cup tapioca in a little cold water and boil: squeeze the juice of two lemons into it, and then add the slices. Eat with cream and sugar when cold.

BREAD PUDDING.
Mrs. Stearns, Madison.

One-third cup butter, two cups sugar, yelks of four eggs, one pint bread crumbs, one quart milk. Stir well and add juice and grated rind of one lemon; beat the whites of the eggs, and stir in two tablespoons pulverized sugar; spread over the top when cold.

FIFTEEN-MINUTE PUDDING.
Mrs. Baggs.

Yelks of six eggs, three tablespoons flour, one pint milk. Work together the yelks and flour; add the milk; beat the whites to a stiff froth; add little salt, and then the beaten whites; bake fifteen minutes. Eat with sauce.

STEAMED PUDDING.
Mrs. Baggs.

One tablespoon baking-powder in one quart flour, a little salt, enough sweet milk to make like muffin batter, one-half pound raisins, seeded. Steam three hours.

SAUCE.

Lump of butter size of an egg, two tablespoons flour, one pint boiling water. Sweeten to taste; add juice of one lemon.

CAKE.

Cake should be made of good materials. It should be baked with a slow, steady heat. Either baking-powder or cream tartar should be sifted in the flour. If soda is used, it should be put in the sour milk, or if with cream tartar, in the flour. To see if the cake is baked, put in a broom-straw; if no dough adheres, the cake is done.

FRUIT CAKE.
Mrs. Haughey.

One dozen eggs, one and one-third pounds brown sugar, same of browned flour, one pound butter, two pounds seeded raisins, two pounds Zante currants, one pound citron, same of figs, one-half pint molasses, one dessertspoon soda, twenty cents' worth cinnamon, one nutmeg.

FRUIT CAKE.
Miss M. E. Knerr.

One pound sugar, one pound raisins, one pound currants, one-fourth pound citron, one pint hickory-nut kernels, three eggs beaten separately, one cup milk, three cups flour, spices to taste, two teaspoons baking-powder in the flour. Flavor; bake two hours.

PORK CAKE.
Mrs. Newton, Cincinnati.

One pound pickled pork chopped fine, two cups boiling water, two teaspoons each of soda, cinnamon, allspice, and cloves, two cups sugar, one pound currants, one-half pound seeded raisins, four and one-half cups flour. Pour the boiling water on the pork.

SCOTCH CAKE.
Mrs. Todd and Mrs. Pattie, Madison.
Work to a cream one-half pound butter with one-fourth pound sugar and two ounces lard, one pound flour, or more, if required to make a stiff dough. Cut in squares, pinch the edges, prick with a fork, and put in bread-pan covered with white paper; bake slowly.

VELVET CAKE.
Miss M. E. Knerr.
Three cups sugar, one and one-half cups butter stirred to a cream, four eggs beaten separately. Add four cups flour with two teaspoons baking-powder; flavor with lemon.

FANCY POUND CAKE.
Repp Brothers, Vienna Bakery.
Three-fourths pound good butter, one pound sugar, ten eggs, one pound flour. Bake in slab; cut cold, any desired shape, and ice the top.

CONFECTIONER'S CAKE.
Beat one-half pound of butter and one-half pound of pulverized sugar to a cream, then add the yelks and whites of eight eggs and two ounces candied orange peel, cut small; add one pound sifted flour and one pound and one-fourth currants, one-fourth pound almonds.

CUP CAKE.
Mrs. Sterns, Madison, Ind.
One cup butter, three cups sugar, six eggs, five cups flour, one cup milk, two teaspoons baking-powder in the flour, grated peel and juice of one lemon.

CORN-STARCH CAKE.
Miss Kittie Lane.
One cup butter, two cups sugar, one cup sweet milk, one cup corn starch, two cups flour, whites of twelve eggs, one teaspoon lemon; two teaspoons baking-powder in the flour.

SPONGE CAKE.
Miss Kittie Lane.

Seven eggs, beaten separately; one pint sugar, one pint flour, one-half teacup water. Beat the yelks and sugar until quite light, then add water and flour; beat hard, then add the whites, and bake slowly one hour.

CHOCOLATE ICING.
Mrs. Irvin.

One cup brown sugar, two ounces chocolate, one tablespoon milk, one-half teaspoon gum arabic dissolved in a little warm water, one-half teaspoon butter; boil ten minutes, stirring, and pour over the cake while hot.

ONE-EGG CAKE.
Mrs. Wiley.

One cup butter, one and one-half cups sugar, one egg, one cup sweet milk, three cups flour, three teaspoons baking-powder, one cup raisins chopped fine.

WHITE SPONGE CAKE.
Mrs. Dr. Gillette.

Whites of eight eggs, beaten to a stiff froth; stir in one goblet of white sugar. Add, gently, one goblet flour, in which is one teaspoon baking-powder. Bake slowly twenty minutes.

PINK MARBLE CAKE.
Mrs. Josephine Pee.

One cup butter, three cups pulverized white sugar, one cup cream or milk, whites of twelve eggs, five cups flour, one and one-half teaspoons baking-powder. Flavor with lemon.

FOR THE COLORING:

One drachm of cochineal, one of alum, one of cream tartar, one of soda; have this prepared by a druggist, and divided into three powders. Color one-half of the cake mixture with one, dissolved in a little water. Use the two kinds of dough in alternate spoonfuls.

WHITE CAKE.

One cup butter, two cups sugar, one cup sweet milk, three cups flour, whites of five eggs, two teaspoons baking-powder.

WHITE CAKE.
Mrs. E. R. Sanders, Greenwood.

Two cups sugar, two-thirds cup butter, one cup milk, three even teaspoons baking-powder in three and one-half cups flour; whites of five eggs; flavor with lemon. Bake one hour in a moderate oven.

FRUIT CAKE.
Miss Kittie Lane.

One cup butter, two cups brown sugar, one cup sour milk, three cups flour, three eggs, one teaspoon soda; one pound each, of raisins and currants; one-half pound citron; spice to taste.

JAM CAKE.
Miss Lyle, Madison.

One cup water or milk; one cup each, of butter, sugar, and molasses; four eggs, four cups flour, three teaspoons baking-powder, one tablespoon mixed spices; one cup of jam or jelly, stirred in; a pinch of pepper, and one of salt. Bake one hour. If desired for pudding, serve warm with sauce.

SPICED CAKE.
Mrs. McWhorter.

Three eggs, one cup sugar, one-half cup molasses, one-half cup butter, two cups flour; one teaspoon each, of cloves and cinnamon; one teaspoon soda, stirred in the molasses; one-half cup each, of coffee, raisins and currants.

HICKORY-NUT CAKE
Mrs. Crane, Chicago.

Two cups sugar, two-thirds cup butter, one cup milk, three eggs, three cups flour, two teaspoons baking-powder, one cup nut-kernels cut fine.

CHOCOLATE MARBLE CAKE.
Miss Mary Page, Madison.

Two cups of coffee sugar, one-half cup butter, two eggs, three and one-half cups flour, one tablespoon baking powder, one cup sweet milk. Flavor with lemon. Dissolve two squares German sweet chocolate in boiling water. Add one-half cup sugar, one teaspoon vanilla, and two tablespoons of the batter. Alternate spoonsful of this dark part with the first batter.

EGGLESS CAKE.
Miss Jessie Wiley.

One and one-half cups sugar, one-half cup butter, one cup sour milk, one teaspoon soda, three cups sifted flour, one-half teaspoon each cinnamon and grated nutmeg, one teacup raisins, chopped and well floured.

LADY CAKE.
Mrs. Enos.

One-half cup butter, one and one-half cups sugar, nearly one cup sweet milk, two cups flour, one and one-half teaspoons baking-powder, whites of four eggs; flavor with almond.

SCOTCH CAKE.
Mrs. Clough.

One cup butter, one cup sugar, four eggs, one cup sour milk, one cup molasses, four cups flour, one teaspoon soda, one large tablespoon spices, one cup raisins or currants. If no fruit is used, add more spices.

ORANGE CAKE.
Miss Lizzie Hackney.

One cup sugar, one-half cup butter, three eggs, one cup cream, three cups flour; grated rind and juice of two large oranges.

ICING.

White of one egg, thickened with sugar.

HOME FRUIT CAKE.
Miss Annie Brown.

One cup butter, one cup sugar, one cup molasses, one small teaspoonful soda dissolved in four tablespoonsful water, four cups flour, one pound seeded raisins kept whole, one-half pound currants, one-fourth pound citron, one teaspoonful each of cinnamon, cloves and nutmeg. Bake two hours in a slow oven. Will keep a year if locked up.

PINK MARBLE CAKE.
Mrs. Foltz.

One cup butter, three cups sugar, one cup sweet milk, five cups flour, whites of twelve eggs, two teaspoons baking-powder in the flour. Flavor.

Powder for Coloring—One drachm each of cochineal, alum, cream tartar, and soda; divide into three powders. Dissolve one of these powders in a third of a cup of boiling water, and stir into one-third of the cake mixture.

COCOANUT LOAF CAKE.
Mrs. S. L. Goode.

Two cups powdered sugar, two-thirds cup butter, one cup sweet milk (including the milk of the cocoanut), whites of five eggs, three cups flour, two teaspoons baking-powder, one large cocoanut grated. Beat butter and sugar together, add milk, then the flour in which the baking-powder has been sifted, alternating with the beaten eggs; lastly, the grated cocoanut; bake one hour in a square pan; frost it and cut in square blocks.

SOFT GINGER-BREAD.
Mrs. Isaac Pattison.

One quart New Orleans molasses, four eggs, one teacup boiling water, one-half cup melted lard, ginger to suit taste; one tablespoon soda in the boiling water. Raisins or currents. Make as stiff as pound cake. Bake in pie-pans.

HARRISON CAKE.

Mrs. Mary Burbridge, Crawfordsville.

One cup butter, one cup sugar, one cup New Orleans molasses, four eggs, one cup sweet milk, one teaspoon soda in water stirred in at the last, one cup raisins, one cup currants, three tablespoons ginger, one nutmeg, one teaspoon each cloves and allspice, flour to make stiff. Bake one hour.

GINGER-BREAD.

Mrs. Rodman.

Three-fourths cup butter, one cup sugar, one cup New Orleans molasses, four eggs, one and one-half teaspoons baking-powder in two pints flour, one cup milk—ginger and other spices.

BREAD CAKE.

Mrs. Enos.

Three cups light dough, one cup and a half sugar, one-half cup lard and butter, four eggs, one cup raisins. Let it rise, and when light, bake. Cinnamon or nutmeg improves this cake.

FIG CAKE.

Miss Lida Wheat.

Two cups sugar, three-fourths cup butter, one-half cup milk, three cups flour, whites of three eggs; three teaspoons baking-powder sifted in the flour. After making two layers from this white dough, add to what is left, cloves, allspice, and cinnamon, one teaspoon each. Add one-half cup molasses: in it, one-half teaspoon soda and one cup flour. This dark dough can be put on as a layer, or can be made as marble cake; spoonsful alternating with the white.

ICING.

Two cups white sugar with the beaten whites of two eggs. Soak one pound figs in boiling water half an hour; split them, and lay thick on the top of the icing, with the seeds down.

FIG CAKE.
Mrs. Emma Alexander.

Light Part—Four cups sugar, one and one-third cups butter, two cups milk, two cups corn-starch, four cups flour, two teaspoons baking-powder, whites of twelve eggs. Flavor with lemon; bake in six layers; let the flour be light measure.

Dark Part—Two cups brown sugar, one cup butter, four eggs, one cup water, one teaspoon soda in water, three and one-half cups flour, one nutmeg, two teaspoons cinnamon, three cups chopped raisins, one pound figs cut lengthwise. Flour the raisins from the measure of flour, and stir into the batter; put into the pans a layer of butter, one of figs, one of batter, and then bake. This will make four layers of cakes. After they are all done, join the white and dark with icing until you have five layers. This will make two large cakes. Very fine.

CHICAGO GINGER-BREAD.

One cup sugar, one cup molasses, one cup sour milk, two-thirds cup butter and lard, one tablespoon ginger, one teaspoon soda in the sour milk, and one teaspoon soda in the molasses; flour enough to stiffen.

SOFT GINGER-BREAD.
Mrs. John McClain.

One pint molasses, one-half cup butter, one egg, one cup sour milk, five cups flour, two teaspoons baking-powder, one tablespoon each ground cloves and ginger.

SOFT GINGER-BREAD.
Mrs. S. L. Goode.

One cup butter, one cup sugar, two cups New Orleans molasses, five cups flour, four eggs, one tablespoonful ginger, one teaspoon soda.

YELLOW CAKE.
Mrs. Foltz.

Yelks of twelve eggs, one cup butter, two cups sugar, one cup milk, three cups flour, two teaspoons baking-powder. Flavor.

SNOW CAKE.
Mrs. Emma Alexander.

One and one-half glasses sifted sugar, one glass flour, one teaspoon cream tartar, one-half teaspoon soda sifted in the flour, whites of ten eggs well beaten.

FRUIT CAKE.
Mrs. Powell Howland.

One pound sugar, one-half pound butter, four eggs, one cup sour cream, one teaspoon soda, four cups flour, one pound raisins, one pound currants, one-half pound citron; one tablespoon each of cinnamon and cloves, and one nutmeg. To cook the raisins, currants and citron in a little water, and then before they are perfectly cool, to dredge them with flour, will prevent their sinking in the cake. Then stir in flour until stiff enough for the spoon to stand in the dough.

GOOD CAKE.
Mrs. J. R. Nichols.

One and one-half pounds sugar, one-half pound butter, four eggs, six coffeecups flour, one pint sour milk, one teaspoon soda. Use with fruit and nuts, if desired.

POUND CAKE.
Mrs. Rodman.

One and one-half cups butter, two cups sugar, seven eggs, one and one-half pints flour, one teaspoon baking-powder. Rub the butter and sugar to a white, light cream; add three of the eggs, one at a time, beating between each addition. Add the flour sifted with the powder. Add lemon or vanilla extract. Mix into a smooth batter and bake in a steady oven. Line pan with buttered paper.

SOFT GINGER CAKE.
Mrs. Mary Kingsbury.

One cup each of sugar, butter, molasses, sour, or buttermilk, two eggs, one teaspoonful soda dissolved in boiling water, one tablespoon ginger, one teaspoon cinnamon. About five cups of flour, enough to make as thick as cup cake. Work in four cups first, and add cautiously. Stir butter, sugar, molasses and spice together, and set on the stove until slightly warm. Beat the eggs light. Add milk to the warm mixture, then the eggs and soda; lastly the flour, and beat very hard. Half a pound of seeded raisins improves this excellent ginger-bread. First dredge them well.

SPONGE GINGER-BREAD.
Mrs. Sappington.

One cup sugar, one cup molasses, one large tablespoon butter, one-half cup buttermilk, two and one-half cups flour, one tablespoon quick yeast, two teaspoons cinnamon and cloves.

WELCOME CAKE.
Miss Crane, Madison.

One and one-half cups sugar, one-half cup butter, three eggs, one-half cup milk, three cups flour, one and one-half teaspoons baking-powder, raisins or currants.

INDIANA CAKE.
Miss Sarah Davison, Madison, Ind.

Two cups sugar, one and one-half cups butter, seven eggs, one cup warm milk, five cups flour, one tablespoon baking-powder.

SPONGE CAKE.
Mrs. Alexander.

One and one-half cups sugar, one and one-half cups flour, seven eggs. No baking-powder; beat together very lightly.

DAISY CAKE.
Daisy Hopper.

One cup butter, two cups sugar, one cup sweet milk, two eggs, two pints flour, two teaspoons baking-powder. Raisins, currants or sliced citron may be added.

WHITE CAKE.
Mrs. A. J. Griffith.

Two cups sugar, one cup butter, one cup sweet milk, two teaspoons baking-powder three and one-half cups flour, whites of five eggs.

CORN-STARCH CAKE.
Mrs. Goodman, Chicago.

Two cups sugar, one cup butter, one cup sweet milk, two cups flour, three-fourths cup corn-starch, whites of six eggs, two teaspoons baking-powder.

HICKORYNUT CAKE.
Mrs. S. H. Crane, Chicago.

Two coffeecups sugar, one coffeecup butter, one coffeecup sweet milk, three and one-half cups flour, one pint hickorynut kernels, one pint raisins, three teaspoons baking-powder, the whites of eight eggs.

WHITE CAKE.
Mrs. Shreve, St. Joseph, Ill.

One cup butter, two cups sugar, one and one-half cups flour, one cup corn-starch with one cup milk, three teaspoons baking-powder in the flour. Add the whites of eight eggs.

TO MAKE ICING FOR CAKES.
Mrs. Rodman.

Two coffeecups pulverized sugar, whites of two eggs. Moisten the sugar, and let it come to a boil. Then stir in the beaten eggs, whipped perfectly stiff, and the juice of one lemon. When stiff enough to fall thread like from the spoon, it is ready to spread.

ANGEL CAKE.
Mrs. Alling, Newark, N. J.

The whites of eleven eggs, one and one-half tumblers powdered sugar, one tumbler sifted flour sifted four times, one teaspoon cream tartar sifted with the flour. Add one teaspoon vanilla. Sift the sugar. Beat the eggs to a stiff froth. Do not stop beating until the batter is put in pan. The pan must not be buttered. Flour the pan. Bake forty minutes and when the cake is done, turn the pan upside down. Do not stir the fire until the cake is done.

ROCK CAKE.

One pint flour, three ounces sugar, and one and one-half ounces each raisins and citron, three eggs, a gill of milk, a teaspoon ginger, three ounces butter and two teaspoons baking-powder. Beat together lightly the whites and yelks of the eggs, add the milk and work all together, until the spoon will stand stiff in the mixture. Slightly flour the pan.

POUND CAKE.
Mrs. Josephine Nichols.

One pound each of butter, granulated sugar, and flour; ten eggs. Work the butter to a cream, pound the sugar and add the eggs. Beat all together twenty minutes, then add the flour.

COFFEE CAKE.
Mrs. George Spahr.

One cup sugar, one cup butter, two eggs, one cup molasses. Add one cup strong, warm coffee, with a teaspoon of soda dissolved in it, four cups flour, one pound raisins stoned and chopped fine, one tablespoon each of cloves, cinnamon and nutmeg. Currants and citron may also be added.

DOVER CAKE.

One pint sugar, one pint flour, three eggs, one-half pint melted butter, one small teacup buttermilk, one small teaspoon soda, nutmeg.

FRENCH CAKE.
Mrs. F. Rubush.

One cup butter, two cups sugar, four eggs, one cup milk, four cups flour, three teaspoons baking-powder.

PLAIN CAKE.

Whites of three eggs, one-half cup butter, one cup sugar, one-half cup milk, two cups flour, one and one-half teaspoons baking-powder.

WHITE CAKE.
Miss Eliza Howard.

Whites of twelve eggs, three cups of sugar, one cup of butter, one cup of milk, four cups of flour, two teaspoons baking-powder. Beat sugar and butter very light. Add the whites, not beaten. Put the baking-powder into the flour and add the milk last.

BUCKEYE CAKE.

One cup butter, two cups white sugar, four cups flour, one cup milk, six eggs, three teaspoons baking-powder.

BEAUTIFUL CAKE.

One and one-half cups sugar, one-half cup butter creamed with it, one cup milk with one teaspoon lemon in it, three cups flour, three teaspoons baking-powder. Add beaten whites of six eggs.

WHITE MOUNTAIN CAKE.

One and one-half cups sugar, one-half cup butter, one-half cup milk, whites of five eggs, one teaspoon baking-powder. Two cups flour.

MEASURE CAKE.
Mrs. Enos.

Two cups sugar, one cup butter, one cup milk, five eggs, three and one-half cups flour. Add to it dredged raisins or currants; three teaspoons baking-powder in the flour.

MARBLE CAKE.
Mrs. Enos.

Dark Part—One cup brown sugar, yelks of five eggs, one-half cup butter, one-half cup milk, one and one-half cups flour.

Light Part—Substitute white sugar and the whites of the eggs. Spice the dark with nutmeg, cloves and cinnamon.

DRIED APPLE FRUIT-CAKE.
Mrs. Enos.

Three cups dried apples soaked over night; drain off the water and cut the size of raisins; simmer, until dry, in two cups molasses. Take one cup sugar, one cup butter well beaten, four eggs, one cup sour milk, one-half teaspoon soda, two teaspoons each of cinnamon, nutmeg and cloves, four and one-half cups flour, one pound each of currants and raisins, one-fourth pound citron. Bake two hours.

FEATHER CAKE.
Mrs. Louise Tousey.

Two cups sugar, one cup sour cream, one-fourth cup butter, three eggs, three cups sifted flour, two small teaspoons of baking-powder. Bake in quick oven. Don't move until done.

SPONGE CAKE.
Miss Bugbee.

Two eggs; whites and yelks beaten separately; one cup of powdered sugar, one cup of flour with one teaspoon baking-powder sifted in; flavor with lemon or vanilla. Lastly, stir in one-half cup boiling water. Bake slowly. Frost, when done, if you please.

SHETBURN CAKE.
Mrs. J. C. French.

Four eggs, two cups sugar, one cup butter, one cup sour cream, one teaspoon soda, one cup raisins, one cup currants, mixed spices. Bake three hours.

QUEEN CAKE.
Miss Bugbee.
One pound white sugar, one pound flour, one-half pound butter, six eggs, one cup milk, two teaspoons baking-powder. Flavor to taste.

MARBLE CAKE.
Mrs. Tousey.
White Part—Whites of seven eggs, two cups white sugar, one cup butter, one cup sweet milk, four cups flour, two teaspoons baking-powder. Flavor with lemon.

Dark Part—Yelks of seven eggs, two cups brown sugar, one cup New Orleans molasses, one cup butter, one cup sweet milk, two teaspoons baking-powder in five cups flour, one teaspoon each of cinnamon, cloves, allspice and nutmeg. Put alternate spoonsful in your pan.

NO-NAME CAKE.
Mrs. Black.
One pint sifted flour, one pint sugar, one pint soft butter, three eggs, one and one-half teaspoonsful baking-powder. Flavor with lemon.

SILVER CAKE.
Miss Janie Crane, Madison.
Whites of four eggs, one cup sugar, one-half cup butter, three-fourths cup sweet milk, one and one-half teaspoons baking-powder, two cups flour.

GOLD CAKE.
Miss Janie Crane, Madison.
Yelks of four eggs, one cup sugar, one-half cup butter, three-fourths cup sweet milk, one and one-half teaspoons baking-powder in two cups of flour.

CUP CAKE.
One cup butter, two cups sugar, three cups flour, four eggs, one cup sour milk, one teaspoon soda.

SPONGE CAKE.
Miss Alma Truax, Madison.

Weight of six eggs in flour, weight of ten eggs in sugar, twelve eggs, yelks beaten well with grated rind and juice of one lemon. Beat the whites stiff. Add sugar. Stir the flour into the yelks, and add the whites and sugar. Line the pan with thin paper. Bake about one hour.

SPONGE CAKE.
Mrs. Wingate.

Four eggs, two cups sugar, two cups flour, two teaspoons baking-powder, one-half teacup boiling water. Flavor.

SPONGE CAKE.
Miss Janie Crane, Madison.

Twelve eggs, one pound of sugar, three-fourths pound flour. Beat the yelks and sugar. Just before adding the flour, stir in one-half teacup warm water; add the beaten whites with the flour.

LADY CAKE.
Mrs. Enos.

Three-fourths pound butter, one pound sugar, three-fourths pound flour, whites of seventeen eggs, and one-fourth pound bitter almonds.

WHITE CAKE.
Mrs. Sarah Root.

The whites of eight eggs, two cups pulverized sugar, one and one-half cups butter, one cup sweet milk, three cups flour, one cup corn-starch, three teaspoons baking-powder. Flavor with lemon.

TENNESSEE CAKE.
Mrs. Dr. Cobleigh, Athens, Tenn.

Yelks of seven eggs and one whole egg, two cups flour, two-thirds cup butter, coffeecup sugar, one small teaspoon baking-powder and one cup milk.

FRUIT CAKE.
Mrs. Hereth.

Beat together one pound white sugar, three-fourths pound butter; mix a glass of grape jelly with one pint of New Orleans molasses, and one pint of milk; stir this mixture into the butter and sugar with one pound of flour (into which sift two teaspoons baking-powder). one teaspoon of lemon, one-fourth ounce of mace; beat the whites of eight eggs separately, and when beaten to a froth, mix them with the cake. Stir well and just before baking, add one pound seeded raisins, one pound currants, and one-half pound citron or almonds. Bake one and one-half hours.

FRUIT CAKE.
Mrs. Hereth.

Four cups brown sugar, two cups butter, six eggs, one cup coffee, seven cups flour, two pounds raisins, two pounds currants, one-half pound citron, one cup molasses, three teaspoons baking-powder. Add spices.

GRAHAM CAKE.
Miss Georgie Howell.

Two cups sugar, three eggs, three-fourths cup butter, two and one-half cups graham flour, two teaspoons baking-powder. Beat eggs separately. Add currants or raisins to suit the taste.

TENNESSEE CAKE.
Mrs. Sehorn, Athens, Tenn.

One cup butter, two cups sugar, three cups flour, one-fourth cup milk, two small teaspoons baking-powder, whites of eight eggs.

SAFFRON CAKE.
Miss Angie Miller.

Four eggs, one-half pound sugar, one-fourth pound butter, a tablespoon saffron, one-half cup water, one pound flour, and two teaspoons baking-powder.

WHITE CAKE.
Mrs. Emma Alexander.

Whites of fifteen eggs, beaten very stiff, six ounces butter rubbed with one pound sugar, one pound flour, three teaspoons baking-powder. Flavor with rose-water. Add three tablespoons ice-water. Delicious.

POOR MAN'S CAKE.
Mrs. S. E. Wagoner.

Two eggs well beaten, one-half cup butter, three-fourths cup milk, two cups rolled sugar, three cups flour through which two teaspoons baking-powder have been sifted. Bake in jelly-tins in a quick oven.

BLACK CAKE.
Mrs. Hammel.

One pound powdered white sugar, three-fourths pound butter, one pound sifted flour, twelve eggs beaten separately, four pounds raisins stoned and chopped, one-half pound citron, cut in thin slices, one-fourth ounce each of cinnamon, nutmeg and cloves. Rub butter and sugar together, add yelks of eggs, part of flour, the spice and whites of the eggs well beaten. One teacup New Orleans molasses darkens the cake and requires no more flour. A layer of batter may be put upon the buttered white paper with which the pan is lined, and next a layer of the dredged raisins and citron, until the pan is two-thirds full. Bake nearly four hours in a slow oven.

SPICE CAKE.
Mrs. Wood.

Two cups brown sugar, one-half cup butter, yelks of five eggs, two teaspoonsful ground cloves, two teaspoonsful allspice, three teaspoons cinnamon, three teaspoons ginger, one nutmeg, one cup sour milk, one and one-half teaspoons soda.

MARBLE CAKE.

White Part—One-half cup butter, two cups sugar, whites of four eggs, one cup sweet milk, one cup corn-starch, one and one-half cups flour, one and one-half teaspoons baking-powder.

Dark Part—One-half cup butter, one cup brown sugar, one-half cup molasses, two eggs, one-half cup cold coffee, two cups flour, one cup raisins, one teaspoon soda, one-half teaspoon each cinnamon, cloves and nutmeg. Bake either as one cake, alternating the spoons of white and dark parts, or in layers.

CUP-CAKE, WITHOUT EGGS.
Miss Crane, Madison.

Two cups sugar, three-fourths cup butter, two teaspoons cream, two cups sour milk with one teaspoon soda, five cups flour, one-half nutmeg, one teaspoon soda. If milk is not sufficiently sour, add one teaspoon cream tartar.

JACKSON CAKE.
Mrs. Newton, Cincinnati.

One-half pound butter, one pound sugar, three-fourths pound flour, seven eggs. Flavor to taste.

FARMERS' FRUIT CAKE.
Miss Wood.

Cut two cupsful of dried apples into small pieces, and soak over night; cook in one pint of molasses; when cold stir in one cupful of butter, one of brown sugar, one of sour milk, one of raisins, one heaping teaspoonful of soda, one nutmeg, one tablespoonful of allspice, one tablespoonful of cinnamon, three eggs, and flour enough to make a very stiff batter.

SPONGE CAKE.
Mrs. Enos.

Five eggs, one-half pound sugar, three-eighths of a pound of flour. Flavor with lemon.

CHEAP FRUIT CAKE.
Mrs. S. L. Goode.

Two cups sugar, one and one-half cups butter, four eggs, one cup sweet milk, one cup molasses, in which dissolve one teaspoon soda; one pound raisins, five cups flour. Spice as you like.

WHITE CAKE.
Mrs. Florence Wood.

Two cups sugar, three-fourths cup butter, whites of seven eggs, one cup milk, two cups flour, one cup corn-starch, two teaspoons baking powder. Flavor with lemon.

JELLY ROLL.
Mrs. Florence Wood.

One cup sugar, three eggs, one and one-half cups flour, two tablespoons cream, one tablespoon baking-powder.

MARBLE CAKE.
Mrs. Florence Wood.

White Part—Two cups sugar, whites of four eggs, three-fourths cup butter, one cup milk, four cups flour, three teaspoons baking-powder.

Dark Part—One cup brown sugar, one-half cup molasses, one-fourth cup butter, one-half cup sour milk, one teaspoon soda, cinnamon, cloves, allspice and lemon.

DELICATE CAKE.
Miss Sallie Irons, Franklin, Ind.

Two cups white sugar, one cup butter. When well stirred, add one cup milk, and then the whites of five eggs beaten light; add two teaspoons baking-powder to four cups flour; stir in flour until the proper consistency. Flavor to taste.

GOLD CAKE.

Yelks of ten eggs, one cup butter, two cups sugar, three cups flour, three-fourths cup milk, three teaspoons baking-powder.

FRENCH CAKE.
Mrs. Rubush.

Two cups sugar, one cup milk, three and one-half cups flour, one-half cup butter, two eggs, two teaspoons baking-powder.

ICE CREAM CAKE.

Six eggs, one pint sugar, one pint flour, one-half teacup water. Beat with the sugar the yelks and one white; add flour, and the whites beaten light.

FEATHER CAKE No. 2.

One cup sugar, three eggs beaten well together, butter the size of an egg, one cup flour, one teaspoon cream tartar mixed with flour, one-half teaspoon soda dissolved in eight teaspoons water. Flavor to taste.

WHITE CAKE.

Whites of ten eggs, two cups sugar, one cup butter, three-fourths cup milk, one-half teaspoon soda, two teaspoons cream tartar, two teaspoons lemon. Cream butter and sugar together; then add the milk and soda; then the eggs and flour in which the cream tartar has been stirred.

CHEAP AND GOOD SPONGE CAKE.

One cup sugar, two eggs, one cup flour, two tablespoons water, one and one-half small teaspoons baking-powder.

MINNESOTA SPONGE CAKE.
Mrs. C. A. Mann.

One cup sugar, one and one-half cups flour after being sifted, five eggs beaten separately, one-half cup water, two teaspoonsful baking-powder. Flavor with lemon.

MRS. PARKER'S GINGER SNAPS.

One pint molasses, one cup brown sugar, one cup butter or sweet lard, three tablespoonsful ginger. Flour enough to mix soft dough. Roll thin and bake quickly.

YANKEE MOLASSES CAKE.
Mrs. J. R. Nichols.

Two cups Orleans molasses, one-third cup butter or sweet lard melted, two eggs, three cups flour, one teaspoonful soda dissolved in one-third of a cup of warm water. Bake as quickly as possible without burning.

OAKALLA'S LADY CAKE.
Mrs. H W. Davis.

One and one-fourth pounds white sugar, one pound butter, one and one-fourth pounds flour, whites of twenty eggs, one teaspoonful soda and two cream tartar, mixed in the flour, or three teaspoonsful baking-powder. Flavor with vanilla. Cream the butter and sugar. Add the flour and eggs alternately, a little at a time. The dough must be pretty stiff. Bake either in a large loaf, or in a square pan, to cut in squares. If iced, will keep moist a long time.

KENTUCKY GINGER BREAD.
Mrs. J. R. Nichols.

Two cups molasses, one tablespoonful butter or sweet lard, (if lard, put in a tiny pinch of salt,) one egg, one cup sour milk, one teaspoonful soda, one tablespoonful ginger, three cups flour. Bake in modern oven. Nice to eat warm for tea, or use as a pudding for dinner with sauce.

ANGEL CAKE.
Mrs. J. E. Springer.

The white of eleven eggs, one cup of flour after sifting, one teaspoon cream tarter. Sift the flour and cream tartar four times. Beat the eggs to a stiff froth, and then beat in one and one-half cups granulated sugar, and a teaspoonful vanilla. Add the flour and beat lightly, but thoroughly. Bake in an ungreased pan, slowly, forty minutes. Cut it out when cool. The pan should be a new one. Let it be turned over and set on the edges of two other pans to cool. The oven should be a slow one. The cake should rise gradually.

MARBLE CAKE.

Mrs. John McClain.

White Part—Two and one-half cups white sugar, one cup butter, one cup sour cream, four cups flour, one-half teaspoon soda. Whites of seven eggs. Flavor to taste.

Dark Part—Two cups brown sugar, one cup molasses, one cup butter, one cup sour cream, one teaspoon soda, four cups flour, yelks seven eggs. Spices of all kinds. Pour the dark part in the pan first.

WHITE CAKE.

Mrs. John McClain.

Whites of five eggs, one and one-half cups white sugar, one of butter, one-half cup milk, two teaspoons baking-powder in three cups flour. Flavor with lemon or vanilla.

FRUIT CAKE.

Mrs. Enos.

One pound butter, one pound flour, ten eggs beaten separately, one pound sugar, two pounds seeded raisins, two pounds currants, one-half pound citron, grated rind and juice of a lemon. Add three teaspoons cinnamon, one of cloves and one nutmeg. Dredge the fruit with flour.

FRUIT AND FEATHER CAKE.

Mrs. McWhorter.

Six eggs, two scant cups sugar, butter twice the size of an egg, two cups flour, three teaspoons baking-powder; mix as usual, and take out rather less than one-half; into this stir one-half pound currants, one-half pound raisins seeded and chopped, two tablespoons sliced citron, one tablespoon candied orange or lemon, one teaspoon grated nutmeg, one of cinnamon, one tablespoon molasses, two cups flour. Bake in jelly-pans; alternate the layers, plain cake first and last the fruit layer, with jelly between and icing outside.

JAPANESE CAKE IN WHITE, RED AND BROWN.
Miss Angie Miller.

Weight of eight eggs in sugar, of six in flour, of four in butter. Add the whites of eight eggs. This makes the white dough. For the red dough, weight of four eggs in red sugar, weight of three in flour, weight of two eggs in butter. Yelks of eight eggs. Take part of the white and part of the red dough, mix together and add one-fourth pound grated chocolate.

SNOW CAKE.
Miss Miller.

Whites of twelve eggs, one-half pound sugar, one-half pound flour, one teaspoon baking-powder. Flavor with lemon.

RIBBON CAKE.
Mrs. Binford.

Two and one-half cups sugar, one cup butter, one cup milk, four eggs, four cups flour, two teaspoons of baking powder. Reserve one-third of this mixture, and bake the rest in two layers. Add to the reserved one-third, one cup chopped raisins, one-fourth pound citron, one cup currants, two tablespoons molasses; one teaspoon each of all kinds of spice. Put the three cakes together with icing or jelly, fruit layer in the middle; frost the top and sides.

CHOCOLATE CAKE.
Miss Kittie Lane.

One coffeecup butter, three of sugar, one and one-half of milk, four of flour, whites of twelve eggs; three teaspoons baking-powder, sifted in the flour. Cream the butter and sugar; add milk and flour, then the eggs. Bake six layers. To the rest of the batter add one cup grated chocolate, and bake also in layers.

FILLING.

Whites of four eggs, two tablespoons white sugar; beat to a stiff froth, and add one cup of chocolate.

HICKORY-NUT CAKE.
Mrs. Enos.

One pound butter, one and one-fourth pounds sugar, ten eggs beaten separately, one pound raisins, one pound currants, one pound chopped hickory-nut kernels, one-fourth pound citron, one-half pint sweet milk, two teaspoons baking-powder in one and one-fourth pounds flour. Flavor with lemon and nutmeg. Bake about two hours in large cake pan. Very fine.

CHOCOLATE CAKE.
Mrs. G. M. Pee.

Two cups sugar, one cup butter, one cup milk, three cups flour, three teaspoons baking-powder, yelks of three eggs and whites of five, beaten separately and stirred in lightly at the last.

DRESSING.

One cup sweet chocolate grated, one pint sugar, one-half cup milk, butter size of an egg; boil ten minutes, then add two teaspoons vanilla. Both cake and dressing should be cold before putting together.

CHOCOLATE CAKE.

One cup white sugar, one-half cup butter, one-half cup milk, one and one-half cups flour, one and one-half teaspoons baking-powder. Add the beaten whites of two eggs, and flavor with lemon.

CREAM ROSE CAKE.
Mrs. Foltz.

Whites of ten eggs, whisked stiff; one cup butter, three cups powdered sugar, one cup cream, nearly five cups of flour, two teaspoons baking-powder; vanilla flavoring. Color with cochineal powder (see Pink Marble Cake), and bake in jelly-tins. When cold, spread with filling of whites of three eggs, whisked stiff, one large cup powdered sugar, and one cocoanut, pared and grated.

NEAPOLITAN CAKE.
Mrs. H. Foltz.

One cup butter, two cups sugar, one cup sweet milk, three cups flour, whites of five eggs, two teaspoons cream tartar, one teaspoon soda. Color one-half of this cake with one-half of one of the powders prepared for pink marble cake. Bake in jelly-tins.

Three-fourths cup butter, two cups sugar, one cup milk, three cups flour, yelks of five eggs, two teaspoons cream tartar, one of soda. Leave half of this yellow, and mix with the other half two tablespoons grated chocolate; bake in jelly-tins. When all done, put together with icing made with whites of three eggs whisked stiff, one heaping cup of powdered sugar, and the juice of a lemon. Lay the brown cake (or chocolate part) first, then the pink, the white, and the yellow.

HARLEQUIN CAKE

Can be made in the same way by putting a large spoon of each color at a time into a pan and baking as a loaf. It can be still further varied by putting powdered pistachio nuts (green, but harmless,) into a part of the white batter.

NEAPOLITAN CAKE.
Mrs. Hackney.

Dark Part—One cup brown sugar, one-half cup butter, one-half cup molasses, one-half cup strong coffee, two and one-half cups flour, two eggs, one teaspoon each of cinnamon and cloves, three teaspoons baking-powder, one-half of a nutmeg, one-half pound each of raisins and currants, and a small piece of citron sliced small.

Light Part—One-half cup butter, two cups white sugar, one cup sweet cream, one cup corn-starch, two and one-half cups flour, three teaspoons baking-powder; four eggs, beaten separately.

FOR ICING:

Two eggs, two cups sugar, grated rind and juice of one lemon.

ALMOND CREAM CAKE.
Mrs. Haughey.

Two cups sugar, six eggs, three cups flour, one-half cup sweet milk, three teaspoons baking-powder, eight tablespoons soft butter. Flavor with vanilla.

FILLING:

One cup sweet cream, whipped; the whites of three eggs well beaten, eight tablespoons pulverized sugar, one pound almonds, blanched and chopped very fine.

ORANGE CREAM CAKE.

Two cups flour, two cups sugar, one-half cup water, the yelks of five eggs and whites of four, two teaspoons baking-powder in the flour, grated rind and juice of one orange.

FILLING:

Beat the white of one egg to a stiff froth, add powdered sugar until stiff, and the juice and rind of one orange.

JOSEPHUS CAKE.
Mrs. Siddall.

Yelk of three eggs, one cup sugar, one tablespoon butter, one teaspoon baking-powder, one-half cup cold water, two cups flour.

FILLING:

Whites of three eggs, one pound sugar, one coffeecup chopped raisins, and chopped peel of one-half orange. Cover top and sides with this frosting.

COCOANUT CAKE.
Mrs. Dr. Wiley.

One-half cup butter, one cup sugar, one-half cup milk, two and one-half cups flour, three eggs (omitting the whites of two), two teaspoons baking-powder in the flour.

FILLING:

Whites of two eggs, one cup sugar, one-half grated cocoanut, four tablespoons sugar, and one-half cocoanut grated on the top.

JELLY CAKE.

Mrs. Bishop, Greenwood.

Three eggs, not separate, one-half cup butter, two cups white sugar, two teaspoons baking-powder, one-half cup sweet milk, three cups flour. Bake in layers and spread with jelly.

CHOCOLATE CAKE.

Mrs. Louise Noble Park, Greenwood.

White Part—Whites of four eggs, one cup sugar, one-half cup butter, one-half cup milk, one and one-half teaspoons baking-powder in two cups flour.

Dark Part—Yelks of four eggs, one cup sugar, one-half cup milk, one-half cup butter, one and one-half teaspoons baking-powder in two cups flour.

Bake in tins; alternate the white and dark parts in the layers.

FOR FROSTING.

Whites of three eggs, one and one-half cups powdered sugar, and two cakes German sweet chocolate.

TEA CAKE, OR LAYER CAKE.

One cup sugar, one-third cup butter, two cups flour, two-thirds cup milk, one egg, two teaspoons baking-powder. Bake in three layers.

JELLY ROLL.

Three cups sugar, one cup butter, five eggs, one cup milk, five cups flour, three teaspoons baking-powder. Bake in thin sheets. Spread with jelly, and roll when cool.

JELLY CAKE.

Five eggs, one cup butter, one cup milk, two cups sugar, three cups flour, three teaspoons baking-powder. Spread the layers with jelly.

LOAF CAKE.
Mrs. Baggs.

Three cups light-bread dough, same of sugar, one cup butter, three eggs, one nutmeg grated, and one large cup seeded raisins. Add spices to taste; mix through the dough; put in pans, and let rise before baking.

GINGER CUP-CAKE.
Mrs. Baggs.

Two eggs, one large cup molasses, one cup butter, one cup brown sugar, one-half cup milk, two and one-half cups flour, one-half cup each of allspice, cloves and cinnamon, one-fourth cup ginger, one teaspoon soda.

BLACK CAKE.
Mrs. Baggs.

Twelve eggs, five cups browned flour, three pounds raisins, same of currants, four cups butter, five cups brown sugar, one cup molasses, three grated nutmegs, two large tablespoons each of ground cloves and cinnamon.

EGGLESS CAKE.
Mrs. John McClain.

Two cups sugar, two tablespoons butter, one cup milk, three cups flour, three small teaspoons baking-powder. Put layers together with cocoanut or jelly, or bake as a loaf cake.

CHOCOLATE CAKE.

One cup white sugar, one-half cup butter, one-half cup milk, one and one-half cups flour, one and one-half teaspoons baking-powder. Add the beaten whites of two eggs, and flavor with lemon.

FILLING:

Whites of two eggs beaten to a stiff froth, one-half cup powdered white sugar stirred in. Grate one-half cake German sweet chocolate and mix with it. If too stiff, add a little cold water.

CHOCOLATE CAKE.
Mrs. Emma Alexander.

Two cups white sugar, one-half cup butter, one-half cup sweet milk, three cups flour, whites of seven eggs, three teaspoons baking-powder. Bake one-half of the batter in jelly-cake pans. In the remaider, grate one-half cake Baker's chocolate, and use as dark layers of the cake. Put together with a thick custard of milk, eggs and sugar.

COCOANUT CAKE.
Mrs. Rodman.

Two even cups powdered sugar, three-fourths cup butter, whites of five eggs, beaten to a stiff froth, one teaspoon soda dissolved in hot water, two teaspoons cream tartar sifted in the flour.

FILLING:

Whites of three eggs whisked stiff, one heaping cup of powdered sugar, one cocoanut peeled and grated. Mix all together, and when cakes are cold, spread with this frosting.

MOUNTAIN CAKE.
Miss Mary Spahr.

Two cups sugar, one half cup butter. yelks of four eggs, whites of two eggs, and one cup milk. three and one-half cups flour, two and one-half teaspoons baking-powder. Put the powder into the one-half cup of flour, and stir in lightly at the last. Flavor with lemon. Take the two whites not used, beat to a stiff froth, sweeten, and use for icing if desired.

DELICIOUS CAKE.
Mrs. Reep, Knoxville, Tenn.

Two cups of sugar, one cup of butter, one cup of sweet milk. three cups of flour, three eggs, one tablespoon baking-powder.

FILLING:

Lemon jelly, made of two lemons grated; one cup of sugar, two eggs, two tablespoons butter; all boiled together until thick. When cool, spread.

COCOANUT CAKE.
Mrs. John McClain.

Two cups sugar, one-half cup butter, three eggs, one cup milk, three cups flour, two teaspoons baking-powder.

FILLING:

One grated cocoanut; to one-half of this add the whites of three eggs beaten to a stiff froth, and one cup sugar; spread this between the layers. Cover the top layer with the remaining grated half of the cocoanut and sugar.

CREAM CAKE.
Mrs. Lowe.

One cup sugar, four eggs, two small cups flour, two teaspoons baking-powder. Flavor to taste.

FILLING:

One egg, two small tablespoons flour, two-thirds pint of milk; sugar enough to sweeten. Cook gently until thick.

LEMON JELLY-CAKE.
Mrs. Lowe.

Two cups sugar, one-half cup butter, one cup milk, three eggs, two tablespoons baking-powder, three cups flour.

FILLING:

Grate the rind of three lemons, add the juice of the same, one egg, one cup sugar, one-half cup water, one teaspoon butter and one tablespoon flour; cook this custard gently until it thickens. It is better made some days before using.

APPLE LEMON JELLY-CAKE.
Miss Lida Wheat.

One cup sugar, one-half cup butter, two eggs, one-half cup milk, two cups flour, one and one-half teaspoons baking-powder.

FILLING:

Grate three large apples and the rind of one lemon, using the juice; add one-half cup sugar, one egg, and a small piece of butter. Cook, and put between the layers while warm.

CORN-STARCH CUSTARD CAKE.
Miss Lida Wheat.

Made in same manner as apple lemon jelly-cake.

FILLING:

One tablespoon sugar, one tablespoon corn-starch, two eggs, and one pint milk; flavor with vanilla. Let it cool before putting between layers.

DELICATE CAKE.
Mrs. Stearns, Madison, Ind.

Two cups sugar, one-half cup butter, whites of five eggs, one cup milk, two and one-half cups flour, two teaspoons baking-powder; flavor. Bake thin, in bread-pans; ice, lay one on another, and cut in squares.

ROCKY MOUNTAIN CAKE.
Mrs. Enos.

Whites of ten eggs, three cups sugar, one-half cup sweet milk, one cup butter, three and one-half cups flour, two teaspoons baking-powder. Flavor with rose.

FILLING:

One-fourth pound raisins, also of citron, almonds, Brazil nuts, figs and one cocoanut. Scald the almonds, after taking off shells, in the water. Dry them thoroughly. Cut them in small pieces. Grate the cocoanut, and cut up figs, currants and raisins. Take the whites of four eggs, one pound pulverized sugar, and make an icing. Spread the layers with the icing and scatter over them the nuts and fruits.

WHITE CAKE.
Mrs. Jennie W. Bass.

Three cups white sugar, one cup butter, one cup sweet milk, four cups flour, three teaspoons baking-powder, sifted in the flour. Whites of ten eggs beaten very light. Work butter and sugar together, add milk, then the flour, and last, the eggs. Flavor with lemon.

VELVET SPONGE-CAKE.
Miss Knerr.

Two cups sugar, four eggs, two cups flour, two teaspoons baking-powder, and one cup hot water.

ICE CREAM FILLING.

Three cups white sugar, one-half cup boiling water. Boil until it makes brittle candy (test by dropping it into cold water); whites of three eggs well beaten; stir into boiling candy; one teaspoon citric acid. Flavor to taste.

MOUNT BLANC CAKE.
Mrs. Fannie Vestal.

Two cups pulverized sugar, one cup butter, one cup sweet milk, four cups flour, whites of eight eggs, three teaspoons baking-powder.

ICING:

Three cups granulated sugar, one pint boiling water. Boil the sugar until it will candy; previously beat the whites of three eggs, and flavor with one tablespoon vanilla; pour the sugar over the eggs and beat until milk warm; the boiling hot sugar may be poured over the well-whipped whites, and the beating continued until nearly cold. Flavor, and spread over the cakes.

JELLY-CAKE ROLL.

Three eggs, one-half cup butter, one cup flour, one and one-half teaspoons baking-powder, two-thirds cup pulverized sugar. Grease a dripping pan, and put in the dough about one-half inch thick; when baked turn it on a cloth, as it will stick to a board, pan or plate; spread jelly evenly and roll while hot.

GINGER COOKIES.
Mrs. Wheatly.

One cup each of sugar, molasses, shortening and boiling water, one teaspoon soda and one tablespoon ginger. Stir all together, and add flour to roll nicely.

GINGER CAKES.
Mrs. H. E. Bishop, Greenwood.

One egg, one quart molasses, five large tablespoons lard, five of boiling water, two of ginger, one of soda. Mix, roll, and cut into cakes.

BUNS.
Mrs. Weyer, Madison.

Two pints of flour, one cup sugar, one cup butter, three eggs, two teaspoons baking-powder. Drop small in pans. One cup of fruit may be added.

COOKIES.
Mrs. Weyer.

Three eggs, whites and yelks beaten separately, one-half cup butter, one and one-half cups sugar, three full cups of flour, and two teaspoons baking powder; flavor with lemon. Cut into round cakes, and bake in a quick oven. Use rind and juice of one lemon.

TAYLOR CAKES.
Mrs. Enos.

Three-fourths pound butter, three-fourths pound sugar, one quart New Orleans molasses, six eggs beaten separately, one pint sour milk, one tablespoon soda, two tablespoons ginger and other spices, three pounds flour. Drop on tins or in gem-pans.

GINGER-SNAPS.
Mrs. Shank.

One pint New Orleans molasses, one pint brown sugar, one cup of butter or salted lard, one teaspoon cloves and cinnamon, one teaspoon soda dissolved in one-half cup warm water, two tablespoons ginger.

COOKIES.
Mrs. Kate Andrews.

Two cups sugar, two eggs, one cup butter, two tablespoons water, one teaspoon soda; roll thin. Bake quickly.

DOUGHNUTS.
Mrs. Bugbee.

Two cups sugar, two eggs, one heaping teaspoon soda, two and one-half tablespoons melted butter, one-half nutmeg, and one pint sour milk. Flour to thicken, and roll out.

SAND CAKES.
Mrs. Norman.

One quart sugar, one quart flour, one pint butter, two eggs, leaving the white of one; roll thin. Spread, with a feather, the beaten white; grate loaf sugar, nutmeg and cinnamon.

GINGER SNAPS.
Miss Mollie Simpson.

One cup lard and butter, one cup sugar, one cup molasses; one-half cup water, one tablespoon each of ginger, cinnamon and cloves, one teaspoon soda dissolved in hot water; flour for stiff dough. Roll thin and bake quickly.

TEA CAKES.
Mrs. L. A. Burleigh.

Three eggs, three cups sugar, three-fourths cup lard and butter, one cup sour milk, one small teaspoon soda. Bake in hot oven.

FOURTH-OF-JULY GINGER CAKES.
Mrs. Kring.

Put into a coffeecup three large spoons melted lard, three spoons water, one teaspoon soda, a little salt, one teaspoon ginger, and fill the cup with molasses. Add flour to thicken, and roll out.

DOUGHNUTS.
Mrs. Erwin.

Two small cups sugar, one cup sweet milk, three eggs, one tablespoon melted butter, three teaspoons baking-powder. Mix with flour as soft as can be rolled out; fry in hot lard.

FRENCH BISCUIT.
Mrs. Black.

Two cups sugar, two cups butter, one egg or the whites of two eggs, one teaspoon baking-powder, flour enough to thicken. Grate sugar on them. There may be used, instead of the baking-powder, one-half cup sour milk, and one-half teaspoon of soda.

ALMOND DOUGHNUTS.
Miss Angie Miller.

One-fourth pound butter rubbed into one quart of flour; add one teaspoon salt, one pound sugar, four eggs beaten, nutmeg, and one-half pint sweet milk; one and one-half teaspoons baking-powder in the flour: roll thin; cut in almond-shape and lay in hot lard; grate white sugar on them.

RAISED DOUGHNUTS.
Mrs. Enos.

One quart sweet milk warmed with one-fourth pound butter and lard mixed, one cup sugar, five eggs beaten light, flour for rather stiff batter, and one cup yeast.

DOUGHNUTS.
Mrs. Enos.

Four eggs, two teacups sugar, one cup butter, one cup sour milk with one teaspoon soda dissolved in it. Beat the butter and sugar; add the beaten eggs, then the milk, and lastly the flour; flavor to taste, with nutmeg, vanilla, lemon, or rose-water; make into soft dough and fry in hot lard.

SAND TARTS.
Mrs. Emma Alexander.

Two pounds flour, one and one-fourth pounds butter, two pounds sugar, three eggs, the white of one beaten light to moisten the tops after they have been rolled out and cut out; sprinkle cinnamon, sugar and pieces of almonds on them.

MOLASSES COOKIES.
Mrs. John McClain.

One cup brown sugar, one cup molasses, one cup butter, two eggs, two tablespoons vinegar, two tablespoons ginger, two teaspoons soda. Add nutmeg, cinnamon and cloves. Let the soda be mixed with the molasses and vinegar. When effervescing, stir into the sugar, molasses, butter and eggs. Add flour to roll out thin.

SAND TARTS.
Mrs. Alexander.

One pound white sugar, five-eighths pound butter, two eggs. Work the butter to a cream with the sugar. Add the eggs. Roll very thin and cut. On the top, sprinkle cinnamon, sugar and almond pieces, after spreading with white of an egg.

MACAROONS.
Mrs. Enos.

Whites of six eggs beaten light, one pound sugar, one pound almonds, beaten in a mortar. Hickory nuts, walnuts or pecans can be used instead of almonds.

JUMBLES.
Miss Belle Reese.

One pound butter, one pound sugar, one pound flour, three eggs, rose-water and cinnamon to flavor.

COOKIES.
Mrs. Hereth.

Two cups sugar, one cup butter, one cup sour milk, one teaspoon soda. Add flour to roll them. Flavor with lemon or nutmeg.

GINGER SNAPS.
Mrs. Spahr, Sr.

One quart molasses, one pound sugar, one and one-fourth pounds butter, ginger, cloves and red pepper to taste. Make stiff and roll thin; bake in a quick oven.

COOKIES.
Mrs. Enos.

One pound sugar, one-half pound butter, two eggs, one cup milk, one pound and a half flour, two teaspoons baking-powder. Flavor with lemon. Drop them off spoon, and sprinkle cinnamon and sugar on them.

TEA CAKES.
Mrs. Noah Clark.

Three eggs, one cup butter, one and one-half cups sugar, one-third cup sweet milk, one teaspoon baking-powder. Flavor with lemon.

DOUGHNUTS.
Hoffman's Bakery.

Three eggs, heaping tablespoon butter, one cup milk, two of sugar, three teaspoons baking-powder, teaspoon cinnamon, one-half nutmeg and flour. Boil immediately in perfectly sweet lard.

CREAM CRULLERS.
Hoffman's Bakery.

Beat two eggs, one cup sugar, and one cup sour cream well together. Add a little salt, one teaspoon soda and flour to make a stiff dough. Boil in perfectly sweet lard. These are very delicious when properly made, but too expensive for bakers to throw on the market.

CREAM COOKIES.
Miss Annie Brown.

One cup sweet cream, one cup sugar, one egg, one heaping teaspoonful baking-powder; sufficient flour to make a soft dough. Roll thin and bake quickly. Season to taste.

WHITE CAKE.
Miss Nora Benson.

One cup butter, three cups sugar, one-fourth cup milk, four cups flour, three teaspoons baking-powder, whites of nine eggs. Flavor with lemon.

CREAM CAKE.
Mrs. Hereth.

Three eggs, one cup sugar, one tablespoon water, one-half teaspoon soda, one teaspoon cream tartar, and one and one half cups flour. Bake in square tin.

CREAM FOR FILLING:

One large cup milk, one egg, one-half cup sugar, butter size of an egg, two heaping teaspoons corn-starch. Split the cake open, and spread on the cream.

ICE CREAM CAKE.
Mrs. Barnes, Lafayette.

Two cups granulated sugar, two-thirds cup butter, two-thirds cup sweet milk, three cups flour, two teaspoons baking-powder, whites of eight eggs.

PINK COLORING:

One drachm cochineal, one drachm alum, one drachm bi-carbonate of soda, one drachm cream tartar. These ingredients should be well pulverized and mixed. Take one teaspoon of the mixture and dissolve in a little water. Take half the batter for the cake and color it with this mixture.

CREAM.

Pour one-half pint boiling water on four cups sugar, and boil until you can take it up with your fingers, when dropped in cold water. Pour the boiling sugar over the beaten whites of four eggs. Stir until it is a perfect cream. Add one-half teaspoon citric acid, and flavor to taste. Put the cream between the pink and white cakes.

RAISIN CAKE.
Mrs. M. C. Johnson.

Two cups sugar, one cup butter, three eggs, one cup cold water, three cups flour, two teaspoons baking-powder, three cups raisins

FILLING:

Make an icing as for ice cream cake, and mix with it hickorynut kernels.

J. K. JAMESON, D. D. S.   W. S. RAWLS, D. D. S.

JAMESON & RAWLS,

DENTISTS,

ROOMS 4 & 5 CLAYPOOL BLOCK,

N. E. Corner Washington and Illinois Streets, opposite Bates House,

Indianapolis, Ind.

SPECIAL ATTENTION GIVEN TO THE PRESERVATION OF THE NATURAL TEETH.

We are provided with the latest and most perfect appliances for administering

NITROUS OXIDE OR LAUGHING GAS,

By which the Gas can be taken with PERFECT SAFETY and the much dreaded operation of having teeth extracted, rendered perfectly painless. COME AND TRY IT.

Being impressed with the idea that a dental office conducted on strictly *business principles*, where first-class operations in all branches of Dentistry could be secured at *reasonable prices*, would receive the endorsement and patronage of the people, we opened an office in this city with full confidence of success, and the very liberal patronage we have received from the citizens of Indianapolis and other parts of the State has assured us that we were not mistaken.

We claim to have had equal advantages and experience with any other dental practitioners in the city, and that our work will compare favorably with the best.

We expect to do First-Class Work and Charge Reasonable Prices.

We do not charge the fancy prices demanded by many good dentists, nor the extremely low prices of incompetent ones who can only secure patronage by low prices. Our motto is first-class work, guaranteeing satisfaction, with charges as reasonable as is consistent with good work.

ARTIFICIAL TEETH

Inserted on all the various materials: Continuous Gum, Gold, Rubber, Celluloid, etc.

Jacob Voegtle,

DEALER IN

STOVES

AND

House Furnishing Goods.

Special Attention given to Furnishing of Kitchens.

A good Cook Stove is a necessity to a household, and the best of them can be found at

S. E. Cor. Washington and Delaware Sts., Indianapolis, Ind.

BEE HIVE PLANING MILL,

73 Pendleton Ave.,

INDIANAPOLIS, - INDIANA.

M. S. HUEY & SON,

DEALERS IN

Lumber, Lath, Shingles,

Fence Posts and Pickets.

MANUFACTURERS OF

Doors, Sash, Blinds, Mantles, Brackets, Flooring, Siding, Molding, Etc., Etc.

☞ FIRST CLASS GOODS AT FAIR PRICES.

S. H. Cobb.   G. F. Branham.

COBB & BRANHAM,

Wholesale and Retail Dealers in

ALL KINDS OF

Coal and Coke.

Best quality, full weight and prompt delivery guaranteed. Telephone Connections.

COAL YARDS:

458 EAST OHIO STRET,
140 SOUTH ALABAMA STREET

——— Principal Office: ———

50 N. Delaware Street,

BALDWIN'S BLOCK,

Indianapolis, Ind.

W. P. CRAFT.   J. MILTON DURY   G. ALEXANDER.

JNO. DURY'S
SHOE PALACE

FINE SHOES, ⇒⋅⋅⇐ LATEST STYLES.
"Common Sense Shoes."

3 East Washington Street,
INDIANAPOLIS.

GEO. J. HAMMEL,
GROCER!

A full line of the Best Goods constantly on hand, at Lowest Prices.

110 and 112 Massachusetts Ave.,
INDIANAPOLIS, IND.

TELEPHONE CONNECTIONS.

Geo. W. Miller.   C. E. Barrett.
Ed. Dickinson.

G. W. MILLER & CO,
CARRIAGE AND WAGON
MAKERS,

Nos. 72, 74, 76 & 78

NORTH DELAWARE ST.
INDIANAPOLIS.

Repairing and Job Work done promptly.

SPICE CAKE.
Mrs. Shreve, St. Joseph, Ill.

One and one-half cups sugar, one-half cup butter, yelks of five eggs, one cup sour milk, three cups flour, one teaspoon each of cinnamon, allspice, cloves and nutmeg, one teaspoon soda in the milk.

BRIDE'S CAKE.
Mrs. Enos.

Three-fourths of a pound of butter, three-fourths pound of flour, one pound sugar and the whites of seventeen eggs Flavor with a quarter of a pound of bitter almonds.

SODA POUND CAKE.
Mrs. M. C. Johnson.

One pound sugar, one pound flour, one-half pound butter, five eggs, one cup milk, three teaspoons baking-powder. This makes two loaves of cake. It is a good recipe for cake pudding.

WHITE MOUNTAIN CAKE.
Mrs. Frank Evarts, Minneapolis.

One and one-half cups sugar, one-half cup butter, one-half cup milk, whites of five eggs, three small cups flour, one full teaspoon baking-powder.

ORANGE CAKE.
Mrs Clough.

Butter size of an egg, two large cups sugar, four eggs beaten together ten minutes, one cup sweet milk, three and one-half cups flour, eight teaspoons baking-powder.

ICING:

Two cups sugar, enough water to keep it from burning; cook until it drops like candy; pour over the well-beaten whites of three eggs. When the icing becomes cold, lay over it slices of oranges

DOUGHNUTS.

Mrs. Evarts.

One cup sugar, one cup sour milk, one-half teaspoon soda, three spoons melted lard. Add flour to make soft dough.

PEACH CAKE.

Bake three sheets of sponge cake. Cut ripe peaches in thin slices and put in layers between cakes. Pour whipped cream over each layer and over the top.

ORANGE CAKE.

Mrs. Scott.

Two cups sugar, eight eggs beaten separately and thoroughly, two cups flour, three teaspoons baking-powder, grated rind of one orange.

WATERMELON CAKE.

Mrs. John Hart.

White Part—Two cups white sugar, one cup butter, one cup sweet milk, three and one-half cups flour, whites of eight eggs, three teaspoons baking-powder.

Red Part—One and one-half cups red sugar, one cup butter, one-third cup sweet milk, whites of four eggs, two cups flour, three teaspoons baking-powder, one cup raisins. Keep the red part around the middle of the pan, and the white at the outer edge.

COFFEE CAKE.

Mrs. Mary Kingston.

Two cups sugar, one cup butter, three eggs, one cup sweet milk, one cup yeast. Add flour sufficient to knead like bread dough. Let rise, and when light roll out in cakes an inch thick. Let rise again, and when ready to bake, rub over with egg or bits of butter, and sprinkle with sugar and cinnamon.

ALMOND SPONGE-CAKE

Miss Rena Newton.

One-half pound sugar, five eggs. Beat the yelks first and add the sugar to them gradually; then beat the whites to a stiff froth and add; sift in flour enough to make a batter of medium stiffness; flavor with almond extract, and before putting in the pan, butter a paper well and line the pan; on the bottom part, put at intervals bits of almond which you have blanched by pouring boiling water over them; after removing the brown skin, cut in small pieces, then pour the batter over until the pan is about half full. Bake for one hour in a slow oven.

NEAPOLITAN CAKE.

Mrs. H. C. Curtis.

Black Part—One-half cup each of butter, brown sugar, molasses and strong coffee; two and one-half cups flour, yelks of five eggs; add one teaspoon each of soda, cinnamon and cloves; one-half pound each of raisins and currants, one-eighth pound citron.

White Part—One-half cup butter, two cups powdered sugar, one cup sweet milk, three-fourths cup corn starch; mix with two and one-half cups flour, three teaspoons baking-powder; add the beaten whites of four eggs. Bake the light and dark parts separately in jelly-cake pans. Spread over the cakes an icing made thus: The white of one egg, the juice of two lemons, and powdered sugar; beat until stiff. This makes three layers of each kind of cake.

WEDDING CAKE.

Mrs. McConnell.

Fifteen eggs, beaten separately, one and one-half pounds butter, one and one-half pounds flour, three pounds seeded raisins, three pounds currants, one and one-half pounds citron, a half pint molssses, one ounce each of ground mace and cinnamon.

CREAM CAKE.
Mrs. McConnell.

One cup sugar, three eggs, one cup flour, one teaspoon baking-powder and one tablespoon butter. Bake in layers.

FILLING:

One pint sweet milk, two eggs, two-thirds cup sugar, two large tablespoons corn-starch and a half cup butter. Flavor with lemon. Cook the cream well and let it cool before putting it in the cake.

COCOANUT CAKE.
Mrs. Frank Martin.

One cup sugar, one-half cup butter, three eggs, two cups flour, two teaspoons baking-powder, one-half cup sweet milk. Beat the butter and sugar together, and the eggs separately.

FILLING:

One egg, three-fourths cup sugar, one-half cup butter, one-half cup flour, one cup dessicated cocoanut, and one-half pint milk, heated to boiling. Spread this over the layers of the cake.

CHOCOLATE CAKE.
Mrs. J. K. Pye.

One cup white sugar, one cup butter, one-fourth cup sweet milk, whites of four eggs, two cups flour, and one teaspoon baking-powder.

FILLING:

Two cups sugar, one-half cup grated chocolate, one cup water. Boil until thick, and then spread.

MADISON CAKE.
Miss Nannie Pye.

Four cups flour, four eggs, one cup butter, one cup sugar, one cup sour milk, one cup molasses, one cup currants or raisins, one large tablespoon spices, and one teaspoon soda. If no fruit is desired in the cake, add more spices.

CUP CAKE.
Mrs. John Hart.
One cup butter, two cups sugar, four eggs, one cup sweet milk, four cups flour, two teaspoons baking-powder.

SPONGE-CAKE ROLL.
Miss Sallie Pye.
Two eggs, one cup sugar, two cups sifted flour, one teaspoon baking-powder, and one-half cup water. Spread and roll while hot.

COCOANUT CAKE.
Miss Kittie Alling, Madison, Ind.
One cup sugar, one-half cup butter, one-half cup milk, three eggs, two cups flour, and two small teaspoons baking-powder.

FILLING:
Heat one-half pint milk and mix with it one cup of grated cocoanut.

ORDER OF MIXING CAKE.
The butter and sugar should first be creamed, or thoroughly worked together; the yelks of eggs should next be added, unless it be fruit cake, when the molasses and soda should be added to the butter and sugar. If milk be used, it should be put in before the yelks of eggs. The whites of eggs should be stirred in last. Fruit should be dredged with flour before stirred in.

SAUCES

OIL SAUCE FOR PICKLES.
Mrs. Baggs.

One-half pint oil, one-half pound mustard, one teaspoon each of cayenne and black pepper, one teacup of celery seed; mix well with strong vinegar. This can be poured over pickles before sealing them in cans.

SAUCE FOR VEGETABLES.
Mrs. Enos.

Boil four eggs hard; rub the yelks smooth with two tablespoons olive oil, two teaspoons made mustard, salt and pepper; one teacup vinegar.

MUSHROOM SAUCE.
Mrs. Baggs.

One teacup sliced mushrooms, four tablespoons butter, one teacup milk or cream, one teaspoon flour, nutmeg, mace, and salt to taste. Stew mushrooms until tender, in barely enough water to cover them. Drain, but do not press them. Add cream, butter, and seasoning. Stew over a bright fire, stirring all the time until it begins to thicken. Add flour wet in cold milk. Boil and serve as gravy.

LEMON SAUCE.
Mrs. Baggs.

One large cup sugar, one-half cup butter, one egg, juice of one lemon and grated half rind, one teaspoon nutmeg, three tablespoons boiling water. Cream the butter and sugar; add the well beaten egg; beat hard ten minutes; add a spoonful at a time of boiling water; put in a tin pail and set in the uncovered top of a tea-kettle. The kettle must be kept boiling until the sauce is very hot. Stir constantly.

LIQUID SAUCE FOR PUDDING.
Mrs. Carter.

One cup sugar, one-half cup butter, two tablespoons flour; smooth the flour in cold water. Stir in boiling water to make one quart of sauce. Flavor with vanilla.

PLAIN PUDDING SAUCE.
Mrs. Lily Bruce.

One tablespoon butter, three teaspoons flour; stir well and add two tablespoons sugar; pour on one pint boiling water. When cool, one beaten egg may be added. Flavor with vanilla.

SNOW SAUCE.
Mrs. Mary Johnson.

Lump of butter size of an egg, one pint of white sugar; beat stiff the whites of three eggs, stir them in the butter and sugar. Flavor with vanilla.

HARD SAUCE FOR PUDDINGS.
Mrs. Springer.

Smooth butter and sugar, one-fourth pound of butter to three-fourths pound of sugar.

BROWN SAUCE.
Mrs. Swift.

Yelks of three eggs, one cup milk, small piece of butter. Boil as custard, and when cool flavor with lemon.

DRAWN BUTTER FOR VEGETABLES.
Mrs. Reynolds.

Rub butter and flour; pour on them boiling water, and serve.

CUSTARDS AND CREAMS.

MERINGUE CUSTARD.
Miss Annie Brown.

One quart milk, four eggs, four tablespoonsful sugar. Let the milk come to a boil, have the eggs and sugar beaten together and stir the boiling milk into them. Put over the fire and thicken without allowing it to boil. Reserve the whites of two eggs; whip with two tablespoonsful powdered sugar, and spread over the top after the custard is poured into a dish. Serve cold.

CUSTARD.

One pint sweet milk, one-half cup white sugar. When boiled, add the yelks of seven eggs and two tablespoons of flour, well beaten, and flavor with vanilla.

CHOCOLATE CUSTARD.
Mrs. Baggs.

Two sections of chocolate cake dissolved in one quart milk, one small cup sugar, yelks of eight eggs, one heaping tablespoon corn-starch; pour the hot milk on the yelks, sugar, and corn-starch, after mixing them smoothly. Leave on the stove a few minutes.

FROZEN CUSTARD.
Mrs. Celia Lester.

Make a custard of one quart milk and one quart cream, six eggs, and three cups sugar. When the milk is almost boiling, stir in the yelks of the eggs that have been beaten with the sugar; then stir in the beaten whites, and stir while the custard boils and thickens.

ICE CREAM.
Mrs. John Duncan.

One quart cream, whites of three eggs, yelks of two eggs. Beat separately; sweeten until very sweet; add one-third teaspoon vanilla.

ICE CREAM.
Mrs. Dr. Wiley.

Three pints sweet cream, one pint powdered sugar, whites of two eggs beaten light, one tablespoon vanilla. Mix thoroughly before putting in freezer.

ICE CREAM.
Mrs. Mary Kingsbury.

To one gallon of cream, take whites of eight eggs; sweeten and flavor to taste. Beat eggs very light, add sugar and cream, and beat again. Freeze some time before using, and let stand with ice surrounding the freezer.

ICE CREAM.
Mrs. Kerper.

One quart cream, one quart new milk, one pound powdered sugar, and the whites of four eggs. Flavor, lemon or vanilla. Freeze.

ICE CREAM.
Miss Zula Wilson.

Two quarts cream, one pound sugar; flavor to taste. Put around the freezer to every three large spoons pounded ice, one spoon coarse salt.

CHOCOLATE ICE CREAM.
Miss Minnie Carter.

One quart cream, three-fourths pound sugar, five tablespoons chocolate, scraped and mixed with the yelks of six eggs. Pour this mixture into the quart of cream, and boil. Flavor with lemon and freeze.

FRUIT ICE CREAM.
Mrs. Duncan.

Same as ice cream. If a juicy fruit, put as much juice as cream.

STRAWBERRY ICE CREAM.
Miss Romie Enos.

Mash in a bowl one quart strawberries with one pound sugar. Add one quart cream, and freeze.

RASPBERRY ICE CREAM.
Mrs. Norman.

Press red raspberries through a seive; pour on them a rich, boiled custard, and freeze.

BANANA ICE CREAM.
Miss Lorena Carter.

Slice bananas, sufficient to flavor the cream—six bananas to one-half gallon of cream. Put the slices into the sweetened cream just before freezing.

LEMON ICE.
Miss Jessie Wiley.

To one pint of lemon juice, add one quart of sugar and one quart of water, in which the rind of three lemons has stood until the water has been flavored. When partly frozen, add the whites of four eggs, beaten to a stiff froth.

STRAWBERRY ICE.
Miss Emma Hutchings.

Take from two quarts of berries their juice; sweeten. Add to this the same quantity of water. Add the beaten whites of three eggs, when nearly frozen, and freeze.

ORANGE ICE.
Miss Ida Norwood.

Add the grated rind of three oranges, the juice of six, and also the juice of two lemons; dissolve one pint of sugar in one pint of cold water. Mix and freeze.

LEMON ICE.
Miss Nellie Hutchings.

Juice of six lemons, two pounds sugar, two quarts water. Freeze.

FROZEN STRAWBERRIES.
Miss Nellie Tetaz.

Mash and freeze the berries; add sugar. Serve with cream.

CURRANT ICE.
Miss Mattie Johnson.

One pound sugar to one pint juice, and one pint water. When partly frozen, add the whites of three eggs.

LEMON FLOAT.
Mrs. Wheatly.

Beat yelks of four eggs, one tablespoon corn starch, one quart milk, and sugar to taste. Stir until it boils, then add one-half teaspoon lemon essence; beat whites of two eggs; sweeten and flavor, and pour on top. Cocoanut may be added to the whites of the eggs.

BANANA CREAM.
Mrs. Mary J. Downey, Irvington.

Dissolve one-half box gelatine in one-half teacup cold water. Put one and one-half cups new milk over the fire, after sweetening to taste. When boiling, pour into it the gelatine. Stir until the gelatine is thoroughly dissolved; then boil ten minutes, and when cold, but not stiff, stir in six bananas, sliced with a silver knife. Mix well, and set away on ice. One hour before using, take a pint of rich cream, sweeten to taste, flavor with vanilla, and whip well. Put the mixture first made into a glass dish, and pour over it the whipped cream.

SPANISH CREAM.
Mrs. J. U. Gregor.

Two ounces gelatine, dissolved in three pints milk; when boiling, stir in the yelks of six eggs; beat the whites of six eggs to a stiff froth with six tablespoons sugar and a half teaspoon vanilla; put together in a bowl and stir well, then turn out on a dish to serve cold.

AMBROSIA.
Mrs. Reynolds.

Slice oranges and mix the slices with grated cocoanut. Sliced pine-apples, oranges and bananas may be used.

SUGGESTIONS.

Custard or cream may be cooked or uncooked before freezing. It may be put in a tightly-covered tin bucket when there is no freezer, and placed in a wooden bucket. The ice and coarse salt should fill the space between the tin and wood. The custard should be stirred after becoming cold, and then left an hour.

DRINKS.

COFFEE.

Keep the coffee box or can covered tight to prevent losing strength of coffee; do not have much coffee browned at once; a small lump of butter stirred through the coffee when browning adds to the richness, and also causes it to brown more evenly. Coffee should be browned often, at least twice a week. Mocha and Java mixed make good coffee; Java and Maracaibo mixed make a lower-priced coffee.

COFFEE.

After the grains are evenly browned, the beaten white of egg, or the whole egg, may cover it. The coffee is to be ground coarse if no sack or seive is used in the coffeepot; very finely ground otherwise, and after mixing in cold water, boiling water should be poured on. For two tablespoonsful of coffee allow one pint of water; after boiling fifteen minutes pour in a little cold water and set aside.

STRAINED COFFEE.

Have in coffee boiler a thin muslin or flannel bag. If it can be tied around the mouth of tin funnel, the lid of coffeepot fitting the top of the funnel, it is excellent. Coffee so made requires no egg and no cold water to be poured in. It is clear and good.

MILK COFFEE.

Make a small quantity of strong coffee with boiling water; have ready as much boiling milk as will be sufficient to add; pour off the coffee into coffeepot and add the boiling milk. Serve immediately, or it will not be good. No cream is required.

TO MAKE BOILED COFFEE.

If egg was not added immediately after browning, mix the ground coffee to be used with a part of the egg, or with the broken shell of the egg, and a little cold water; have the boiler well scalded, and pour boiling water on this mixed coffee; only pour one-half as much water as is needed, that it may not boil over. Let it boil five minutes, stirring it down once, and then add the required boiling water.

COFFEE FROM COLD WATER.

To one pint of cold water put two tablespoons coffee; it need not boil, but should come to boiling point and be kept very hot and simmering for fifteen minutes. The egg or shell should be mixed with the coffee before heating. One-half teacup cold water should be quickly poured into coffee boiler when taking it from stove, unless the coffee is to be poured off into a coffeepot.

TEA.

Scald the teapot; pour in boiling water, and afterward the tea, that the leaves may swell; put two teapoonsful of tea to one pint of water.

CHOCOLATE.

Use powdered chocolate, one-half cup to one pint boiling water. Boil twenty minutes; add one pint milk and boil five minutes more; sweeten when boiling.

SUGGESTIONS.

When cream is not obtainable, by scalding the milk and adding it while hot to the coffee, the absence of cream will not be noticed. The sugar and cream should be put in the cup before pouring the coffee. The milk or cream should be put in the cup of tea before it is poured.

CHILDREN'S TEA.

Boiling water and milk in equal proportions.

LEMONADE.

One quart of water; use two lemons; slice them and press with a potato-masher if a lemon-squeezer is not available; add five tablespoons white sugar; the water should be very cold.

HOT LEMONADE.

After pressing the slices of lemon, pour on boiling water. When drank at night an excellent remedy for cold, and at any time good for rheumatism.

WARM MILK.

This should be used in small quantities and at short intervals for weakness, especially in cases of diarrhœa; the milk should not be heated to the boiling point. Another way is to boil the milk, and add pepper and salt.

INVALID'S DRINK.

Beat up an egg in a glass of lemonade.

GRUEL.

Corn meal, oat meal or arrow root may be used; first smooth with cold water, as for gravy; pour one pint boiling water on one-half cup of the paste.

BEEF TEA.

Put one pound minced beef in one pint cold water; boil fifteen minutes and drain thoroughly; season the tea with pepper and salt.

INFANT'S FOOD.
Mrs. Van Wagenen, Orange, New Jersey.

Gelatine, five grains; arrowroot, twenty-five grains; water one and a half pints. These quantities are always to be used; the milk and cream are to be increased with the age of the child.

Milk, two gills; cream, one gill.

For the first three months, milk, three gills; cream, one gill.

From three to six months, milk, one pint; cream, one and a half gills.

From six to nine months, milk, one and one-quarter pints; cream, one and one-half or two gills.

From nine to twelve months. If the child should be feeble, make the water one quart.

Put one and one-quarter pints of water in a sauce pan over the fire, and dissolve the gelatine in it. When the water boils, pour in the arrowroot, previously mixed with a gill of cold water. Let this boil five minutes, then add the milk; when that boils, pour in the cream, and remove it immediately from the fire. Sweeten it with loaf sugar, a little sweeter than good cow's milk. The milk should come from one good cow, and the cream should be not more than three or four hours old. If the child is constipated, use more cream; if otherwise, less should be used. Two quarts of milk will furnish the cream that is necessary, and yet be good for family use. Be careful to measure out the specified quantity of milk while it is new, and set it by itself. In cold weather, if you take milk of a milkman, make it bloodwarm before setting it away, else it will be difficult to get the cream in the specified time.

The above recipe has undoubtedly saved the lives of many babies.

CANNING FRUIT.

Tin cans are liable to become corroded by the action of the acid in the fruit upon the tin, and if the inside is discolored, the can should not be used the second time. Glass, self-sealing cans are now generally used by housekeepers. There is no danger of breaking the glass if it is set on a cold, wet dish-cloth, or towel, in a pan. A silver spoon in the can, or a long carving-knife, is also a good protection. Fruit should be well cooked. If not "done through," it will not keep. The color is lighter and fresher if only a small quantity of fruit is cooked at a time. The jelly is a brighter color if only one or two glasses are made at a time. If the tumblers have not glass tops, it is well to put them under glass until the jelly cools, and the moisture can be wiped off the glass. Cans should be turned upside down, so that after contraction, the tops can be tightened. The following is a good time-table for boiling fruit:

Time for Boiling, and Quantity of Sugar to one Quart Fruit.

	Minutes.	Ounces.
Cherries	5	6
Raspberries	6	4
Blackberries	6	6
Strawberries	8	8
Plums	10	10
Whortleberries	5	8
Pieplant, sliced	10	8
Small, sour pears, whole	30	4
Bartlett pears, halved	20	6
Peaches	8	4
Peaches, whole	15	4
Pineapples, sliced	15	6
Siberian crab apples	25	8
Sour apples, quartered	10	5
Ripe currants	6	8
Wild grapes	10	8
Tomatoes	20	2
Gooseberries	8	8
Quinces, sliced	15	10

PRESERVES.

WATERMELON PRESERVES.
Mrs. Baggs.

Dissolve one ounce of alum in one half gallon water. Scald the melon rinds until tender; add one cup vinegar, and stew the rinds slowly until green. After this, soak in cold water one hour, changing the water often. Make a syrup of one quart of white sugar and three-fourths of a pint of vinegar. Season with ginger, cinnamon, lemon and mace. Pour over the rinds, scalding hot, for three or four mornings.

SPICED GRAPES.
Mrs. McConnell.

Squeeze the pulps from the skins. Cook them until tender; put them through the colander to remove seeds; then cook the pulps and skins together. Take seven pounds grapes, three pounds sugar, one pint vinegar, and spice to taste. Boil until the grape skins are tender and the mixture thick.

CITRON PRESERVES.
Mrs. Clough.

Prepare the rind by soaking twenty-four hours, or longer, in salt water, and then in clear water, changing it several times a day. Alternate layers of rind and grape leaves in a kettle, beginning with the leaves, and sprinkling a little alum on each layer. After scalding well, scald again in clear water to remove the alum taste. Then boil in ginger water, and to every pound of fruit, put one and one-fourth pounds of sugar and one pint of water. Add mace and cinnamon to taste. The fruit must be weighed before putting in salt water.

GRAPE BUTTER.
Mrs. Enos.

One-half pound sugar to one pound grapes. Boil the pulps; squeeze through a colander, and add the skins. As soon as tender, put in the sugar and boil.

CRYSTAL JELLY.
Mrs. Baggs.

One box Cox's gelatine; dissolve it and four coffeecups sugar in one pint boiling water; add the juice of four lemons; stir well until dissolved. Put in a cool place until it begins to congeal, then stir in the well-beaten whites of two eggs; when thoroughly mixed, put in moulds and let stand. Serve with whipped cream or a boiled custard.

GRAPE JELLY.
Mrs. Baggs.

One box Cox's gelatine; dissolve it in two tumblers of cold water; add the grated rind and the juice of four lemons, two pints of white sugar, and one and one-half tumblers grape juice; stir well; add five tumblers boiling water. Strain, and set to cool.

SWEET PICKLES.
Mrs. Baggs.

Seven pounds fruit, four pounds sugar, one pint vinegar, one-half tablespoon mace, two tablespoons cinnamon, one teaspoon cloves. Boil until the fruit is tender, and seal up in cans.

VIRGINIA SWEET PICKLES.
Mrs. Baggs.

Two gallons cider vinegar, two pounds brown sugar, one pint mustard seed, five ounces ginger, three ounces each of black pepper and allspice, one ounce each of mace, celery seed, and tumeric; add one handful of garlic, and one large horseradish, scraped. Mix, set in the sun, and stir frequently before putting the pickles into the mixture.

WATERMELON SWEET PICKLES.
Mrs. Craig.

Take the white part of two melons and cut in squares and scald in salt water; let stand three hours and then drain until dry; one and one-half ounces each of cinnamon and mace; boil three cups sugar and one cup vinegar into a syrup for nine mornings, and pour over the melon each time—warm, but not hot.

CITRON PRESERVES.
Mrs. S. J. Meginnis.

Slice the citron and take out the seeds, leaving all the meat; let it lay in white sugar over night, and in the morning take the melon out of the syrup; let the syrup come to a boil and drop on the fruit; cook the preserve until the syrup thickens.

PEACH PICKLE.
Mrs. Flora.

One pint of sugar to one quart of vinegar. Boil nine mornings, and on the ninth heat all together.

CLING-PEACH PICKLE.
Mrs. Craig.

Three pounds sugar, seven pounds peaches, one pint vinegar, two ounces cinnamon, two grated nutmegs, two or three cloves put into each peach. Boil the vinegar and spices and pour over the fruit hot; pour over every other morning for nine mornings.

WHOLE BAKED APPLES.

Cut out the core, and fill with sugar, butter and cinnamon. Put a little water in the pan.

SPICED PEACHES.

Eight pounds peaches, four pounds sugar, one pint vinegar, and spice to taste. Cook and seal immediately.

SWEET-PICKLED CUCUMBERS.
Mrs. Flora.
Let them soak over night in a weak brine; heat them well (to a boil) in vinegar; add sugar, cayenne pepper, and boil them; seal them while hot.

PRESERVED PEACHES.
Mrs. McWhorter.
Seven pounds fruit, one quart vinegar, four pounds sugar, one ounce unground cinnamon, pinch of cloves, nutmeg and allspice, three tablespoons lemon extract. Tie spices in thin cloth; put in the vinegar and sugar; after boiling a few minutes take out the peaches; keep the juice boiling and put the fruit in and out several times; lastly, boil the fruit and juice until the juice becomes thick.

SWEET PICKLES.
One gallon strong vinegar, four pounds brown sugar, one gallon fruit, cloves, cinnamon and allspice to taste. Simmer fruit gently until done enough to run a straw through; take out and pack in a jar; boil syrup until moderately thick, then pour over the fruit. If you have more syrup than you can use, cut a few more peaches, throw them in and cook awhile. They will do for present use.

BAKED APPLES.
Miss Lida Wheat.
Peel and quarter one dozen good apples. Mix one tablespoon flour and two tablespoons sugar; grate on them a little nutmeg. Pour in enough cold water to half cover the apples. Stir up well, put in the apples and bake in a hot oven.

STEWED APPLES.
Pare and quarter good stewing apples; put in a baking dish, cover thickly with sugar; bits of lemon peel may be added. Cover with a plate, and bake in the oven—in a pan of hot water.

RHUBARB, OR PIE-PLANT.

Stew with sugar, putting a very little water in the kettle. An excellent sauce, especially for spring.

STEWED APPLES.
Mrs. Emma Able, Franklin.

Make a syrup of water and sugar. When boiling, put in quartered apples. They ought not to break.

STEWED FIGS.
Mrs. Rickert.

Put one pound in stew pan with water to cover. Let them simmer an hour, Squeeze in the juice of two or three lemons. Eat hot or cold. No sugar.

CRANBERRY JELLY.
Mrs. Black.

Two quarts cranberries; add one pint of cold water; stir occasionally over a quick fire until the berries are soft; mash, boil, and add one quart sugar; boil ten minutes and pour into mold. Let the berries be on the fire no more than twenty-five minutes.

CURRANT JELLY.
Mrs. J. E. Springer.

Wash the currants, strain them, and then put pound to pound, or pint to pint, of the juice and sugar. Boil twenty minutes, or, boil ten minutes before straining and fifteen minutes after.

PLUM JELLY.
Mrs. Reynolds.

Put them in oven to burst the plums, and then make the jelly "pound to pound."

GRAPE JELLY.
Mrs. Enos.

Green grapes make a beautiful jelly. Boil fifteen minutes alone; add sugar, and boil five minutes.

APPLE JELLY.
Mrs. Hereth.

Belleflower, Crab, or Rambo apples make good jelly. Cut up the apples and put enough cold water to cover them; boil them soft, strain, and then boil twenty minutes. Don't strain so close but that you can add a little water and make an apple sauce.

Quince jelly is made the same.

GELATINE JELLY.
Mrs. Bugbee.

Dissolve one ounce gelatine in one pint cold water; add the rind and juice of two lemons, and one pound of sugar; pour over all one quart boiling water; add lemon, orange, or raspberry juice. Pour into a mould.

Blackberry and raspberry jelly are made as currant jelly.

GRAPE JAM.
Mrs. Rubush.

Separate the skin from the pulp. Heat the pulp in water, and strain out the seeds; put the skins with the seeded pulp, and to each pound add three-fourths of a pound of sugar. Add sufficient water to prevent burning. Cook slowly one hour.

BLACKBERRY JAM.
Mrs. L. A. Burleigh.

Three-fourths pound of sugar to one pound of berries. Cook and stir about one hour.

RASPBERRY JAM.
Mrs. Celia Lester.

Use red raspberries, and equal quantity of good white sugar.

QUINCE JAM.

Boil the quinces soft; pour off the water and mash, then add equal quantity of sugar, and stir while cooking.

CANDY.

CANDY.
Mrs. Lily Bruce.

Three teacups white sugar, one and one-half teacups sweet milk. Boil until hard. Flavor with vanilla. Stir constantly.

BOSTON CHOCOLATE CARAMELS.

One pint grated chocolate, two pints brown sugar, one pint molasses, one-half cup milk, butter size of an egg, vanilla flavor. Boil about twenty-five minutes. Pour into buttered tins; when partly cool, mark in deep squares with a knife.

CHOCOLATE KISSES.
Miss M. E. Kneer.

One cake Baker's chocolate, one pound granulated sugar, whites of five eggs. Beat the eggs to a stiff froth, mix the chocolate and sugar. Drop on a buttered pan, and set in oven long enough to harden.

CHOCOLATE CARAMELS.
Mrs. Enos.

Two cups white sugar, four spoons molasses, one small cup milk, butter size of a large egg, and one quarter pound chocolate. Boil about twenty minutes; flavor with vanilla.

COCOANUT CARAMELS.
Mrs. Enos.

One-half pint milk, one and one-half ounces grated cocoanut. Let the milk boil. Stir in the cocoanut. Add one-half pint white sugar and two tablespoons molasses; pour when thick, in buttered pans; cut in squares.

MOLASSES CANDY.

One cup sugar, one teaspoon butter, one tablespoon vinegar, one cup water. Let it boil thirty minutes; when cold, break in pieces.

CARAMEL CAKE.
Mrs. Rev. Brown, Madison, Ind.

Two cups sugar, one cup molasses, one tablespoon butter, three tablespoons flour. Boil twenty-five minutes; then stir in half pound grated chocolate wet in a half cup sweet milk, and boil until it hardens on the spoon, with which you must stir it frequently. Flavor with a teaspoonful vanilla.

COCOANUT CANDY.
Miss Jessie Wiley.

Two pounds fine white sugar, whites of two eggs; mix this with the grated meat and milk of one cocoanut. Let dry in a warm place, having formed into little flat cakes, and placed on buttered paper.

SUGAR CANDY.
Mrs. Woodburn.

One quart brown sugar, one pint water, two tablespoons vinegar, butter size of an egg, one-half teaspoon soda. Don't stir, or let it get too hard. Pull without twisting.

CHOCOLATE CARAMELS.
Miss Sanxay, Madison.

Three pounds brown sugar, one cup Baker's chocolate, one cup milk, butter size of an egg. Put all together and boil in little water. Must not be stirred.

FIG CANDY.
Miss Clough.

One pound sugar, one pint water; boil on a slow fire, and when done, add a small piece of butter and a few drops of water. Turn it on split figs. Do not boil as hard as for common sugar or molasses candy.

BUTTER-SCOTCH.

One cup New Orleans molasses, one cup butter, one and one-half cups sugar. Boil until it snaps when dropped into water.

SUGAR CANDY.

One pound sugar, one-half pound butter, two tablespoons vinegar, with water enough to dissolve the sugar. Flavor with vanilla. It must not be stirred.

COCOANUT PUFFS.

Beat to stiff froth the whites of three eggs, add two cups granulated sugar, two teacups grated cocoanut. Drop on pans, and bake quickly.

HICKORY NUT CANDY.
Miss M. E. Knerr.

The whites of two eggs, one pound of granulated sugar, one tablespoon flour, one pound of nut-kernels, chopped fine. Beat the eggs to a froth. Drop on tins.

CHOCOLATE CARAMELS.

One cup sweet milk, one cup molasses, one-half cup sugar, one-half cup grated chocolate, small piece butter; stir constantly until thick; turn upon buttered plates. When beginning to stiffen, mark into squares.

COCOANUT CARAMELS.

Two cups grated cocoanut, one cup sugar, two teaspoons flour, the whites of three eggs, beaten stiff. Bake on a buttered paper in a quick oven.

CHOCOLATE CANDY.
Mrs. Hereth.

One-half pound chocolate, one and one-half pounds brown sugar, three-fourths cup milk. Grate the chocolate; mix with sugar and a little water. Put the milk on stove, and just before it boils, stir in the mixture.

TAFFY.
Mrs. Hereth.

Six cups white sugar, one cup vinegar, one cup water; when nearly boiled enough, add one tablespoon butter and one teaspoon baking soda, dissolved in hot water. Boil without stirring one-half hour, or until it crisps in cold water.

NUT CANDY.

To one quart New Orleans molasses, one cup sugar, one-half cup vinegar and one-half cup butter, add one teaspoon soda. Butter the pans, and when candy is sufficiently boiled, pour it over the kernels of nuts—hickory-nuts, butternuts, pecans or peanuts.

MISCELLANEOUS.

DON'T DO IT.—*Foote's Health Monthly* gives the following good rules:

Don't sleep in a draught.

Don't go to bed with cold feet.

Don't stand over hot air registers.

Don't eat what you do not need just to save it.

Don't try to get cool too quickly after exercising.

Don't sleep with insecure false teeth in your mouth.

Don't start the day's work without a good breakfast.

Don't sleep in a room without ventilation of some kind.

Don't stuff a cold lest you be next obliged to starve a fever.

Don't try to get along with less than eight or nine hours' sleep.

Don't try to get along without flannel underclothing in winter.

Don't use your voice for loud speaking or singing when hoarse.

Don't sleep in the same undergarments you wear during the day.

Don't neglect to have at least one movement of the bowels each day.

Don't toast your feet before the fire, but try sunlight friction instead.

Don't drink ice-water by the glass; take it in sips a swallow at a time.

Don't eat snow to quench thirst; it brings on inflammation of the throat.

Don't try to keep up on coffee and alcohol when you ought to go to bed.

Don't strain your eyes by reading or working with insufficient or flickering light.

Don't use the eyes for reading or fine work in the twilight of evening or early morn.

Don't try to lengthen your days by cutting short your night's rest; it is poor economy.

Don't wear close, heavy fur or rubber caps or hats if your hair is thin or falls out easily.

Don't eat any thing between meals excepting fruits or a glass of hot milk if you feel faint.

Don't take some other person's medicine because you are troubled somewhat as they were.

TO CLEAN WHITE PAINT.

Add ammonia to the soap and water, and wipe off with a rag.

GOOD INK.

One half drachm bi-chromate of potash, one-half drachm prussiate of potash, and one ounce extract logwood. Boil the logwood in two quarts soft water. Add the other ingredients and the ink will not mould.

GOOD CEMENT.

Mix glycerine and litharge to consistency of fresh putty. With this cement you can mend dishes, pans, lamps and loose nuts.

TO DESTROY CABBAGE WORMS.

Sprinkle early in the morning with warm wood ashes. Cayenne pepper dusted over them is also destructive.

FOR POTATO BUGS.

One teaspoon Paris green to twelve quarts water.

FOR SICK CHICKENS.

One teaspoon, or less, according to the chicken's age, of melted lard.

TO PRESERVE EGGS.

Cover them lightly with melted tallow, and pack in sawdust.

TO BLACKEN GRATE, OR IRON MANTLE.

Mix sugar and vinegar in a teacup, and apply with a rag.

TO CLEAN BLACK CRAPE.
Mrs. Haughey.

To a half cup warm water, add a few drops ammonia; dip a small piece woolen cloth in the water and rub with the grain of the crape; lay the pieces on black goods and press between blankets until dry. The crape will then look fresh and new. If the material is the best, it can be done up several times.

TO CLEAN WHITE FURS.
Mrs. Haughey.
Rub through them thoroughly, dry corn meal.

TO CLEAN BLACK CLOTH.
Mix ammonia, alcohol and ether; one-fourth as much ammonia as alcohol, and one-half as much ether as ammonia.

TO REMOVE RUST FROM IRON OR STEEL.
Dissolve one teaspoon potash in one gallon boiling water; dip in the rusty article, wash and wipe dry.

TO REMOVE IRON-RUST OR INK STAINS.
Oxalic acid dissolved in warm water.

TO REMOVE FRUIT STAINS.
Pour boiling water through the cloth, or wash in milk, before wetting with water.

TO REMOVE BLOOD STAINS.
Cover thick with starch and put in sun, or wet with alcohol, rub with soap and wash in cold water.

TO REMOVE OIL FROM A CARPET.
Scatter corn meal or powdered chalk, and let remain until the oil is absorbed. Saw-dust has same effect.

TO REMOVE INK.
Dip the cloth in milk, or melted tallow. Then wash.

TO REMOVE GREASE FROM WALL-PAPER.
Lay folds of blotting paper over the spot and hold a hot iron on, to absorb the grease.

TO RENEW BLACK GRENADINE.
Mrs. Black.
Sponge the goods with indigo water, and iron. It blackens and stiffens.

TO CLEAN SILK.

Mix one-half cup each of ox gall, ammonia and soft water.

TO REMOVE ODORS.

Throw ground coffee on a pan of hot coals.

TO MAKE STARCH.
Mrs. Arndt.

Smooth three tablespoons starch in cold water. Pour into one quart of boiling water. Put in one teaspoon each of coal oil and loaf sugar, and a pinch of salt. Boil one-half hour.

TO REMOVE MILDEW FROM LINEN.

Rub with soap, and then scrape chalk upon it. Lay on the grass, and as it dries, the stain will disappear.

TO MAKE SOAP.

Twelve gallons water, two and one-half pounds lime and five and one-half pounds soda ash boiled together one hour. Then add twelve pounds grease, and let all boil until sufficiently thick.

TO DESTROY INSECTS.

Dissolve one pound alum in two quarts boiling water. Apply to every crevice. It leaves no odor nor stain, even upon the carpet.

TO DESTROY BEDBUGS.

Mix one ounce corrosive sublimate in one pint spirits of turpentine. One ounce gum camphor may be added. Poison.

TO DESTROY MOTHS.

Rub a wet towel spread over suspected parts with a hot iron. The steam will kill the moths.

TO DESTROY ANTS.

Lobelia seed or elderberry branches. Cucumber rinds will destroy roaches.

A chalk line around sugar box or barrel will stop ants.

Tar is very offensive to insects. Tar paper will protect furs. Tar in whitewash will keep off insects and cure chicken cholera if used on fences and walls of hen-houses.

TO KILL ROACHES.

Mix equal parts of red lead, corn meal and molasses. Put the mixture on iron plates, such as stove lids, and set it where roaches come.

Pulverized borax will banish roaches.

Cloves scattered where there are red ants, will drive them all away.

TO WASH GREASY POTS AND KETTLES.

First take a handful of meal and rub around the inside. It absorbs the grease.

TO PRESERVE GUMARABIC.

Put in a few drops of oil of cloves.

Soda will remove spots from tableware.

Soiled clothes may be put in soap-suds, but never in hot, clear water.

Black pepper sprinkled over furs in box, and then the box wrapped in paper or cotton bag, will effectually prevent moths.

Stand the kitchen safe in cans of water, and there will be no trouble from ants.

CURE FOR HOARSENESS.
Mrs. Reakirt.

Bake a lemon, or an orange, twenty minutes; open one end; take out the inside; sweeten with sugar or molasses. A sure cure for a cold.

FLAXSEED LEMONADE.
Mrs. M. E. Knerr.

Four tablespoons flaxseed, one quart boiling water poured upon the flaxseed, and the juice of two lemons. Sweeten to taste; steep two hours in a covered pitcher; if too thick, put in cold water.

FOR A COLD.
Mrs. I. N. Pattison, Sr.

Drink a glass of cold water in which has been stirred a half teaspoon of cayenne pepper.

TO REMOVE STAINS FROM MARBLE.

Oil of vitrol and water, or oxalic acid and water. A paste of whiting and potash may be put on grease spots. When rubbed off, the grease is gone.

CURE FOR SMALLPOX.

Sulphate zinc, one grain; foxglove (digitalis), one grain; one-half teaspoon sugar. Mix with two tablespoons water. Take one spoonful every hour. Either scarlet fever, or smallpox cured in twelve hours. For a child, smaller doses.

SCARLET FEVER.

Three tablespoons sweetened water; good brewer's yeast, one tablespoon. Give three times a day. If throat is swollen, make a poultice of the above with Indian meal, and gargle with the yeast. Keep the eruption out by drinking catnip tea freely.

The above recipe is good for smallpox, with milk diet. It seldom leaves a pox-mark.

TO PREVENT SMALLPOX PITTING.

Bi-sulphate soda, two drachms; fresh glycerine, one ounce; carbolic acid, one scruple.

TO KEEP OFF RATS.

Grow wild peppermint.

FOR CHAPPED HANDS.

Equal parts spirits of camphor, glycerine, ammonia and rain-water.

FOR SORE THROAT.

Gargle with salt, water and vinegar. Put on the outside a slice of fat bacon.

FOR SICK HEADACHE.

One teaspoon powdered charcoal in one-half glass of water. Another good remedy is to dissolve a small piece of gum camphor in the mouth—but too much would be very injurious.

FOR DIPHTHERIA.

Put sulphur in water and gargle with it. If some is swallowed it will do good.

INGROWING NAILS.

Burn with caustic. Severe, but sure. Another remedy is to scrape the top of the nail thin with glass, and this will make the corners turn up and grow flat.

FOR CONSUMPTION.

Mullen leaves distilled in water and a syrup made with granulated white sugar and the liquid. If the cough is troublesome, drink freely and often, mullen tea.

FOR CONSUMPTION.

Take a teaspoon of the juice of hoarhound, and mix it with a gill of new milk. Drink it warm. It is a wonderful cure, if persevered in.

FOR RHEUMATISM.

Lemon juice in warm water two or three times a day.

FOR CROUP.

Beat the white of an egg to a stiff froth, and sweeten. If a severe case, rub the chest with camphor and lard.

FOR WHOOPING COUGH.

Equal parts goose grease and honey—a teaspoonful for a dose.

FOR CORNS AND WARTS.

Apply acetic acid every day. Another remedy—mix two tablespoons each brown sugar, saltpeter and tar. Warm the mixture and spread on leather size of corn, and in a few days the corn will come out.

CURE FOR FELON.

In the beginning, immerse in lye, as hot as can be borne, for half an hour at a time. Apply a plaster of salt, soap and turpentine. If it comes to a head, lance it and poultice with lye and elm bark. Heal with a salve made of resin and tallow, two ounces of each.

Another good remedy is, bathe the finger in ashes and water. Take the yelk of an egg, six drops of turpentine, a few beet leaves cut fine, a little hard soap, and a teaspoon of snuff or fine tobacco; add one tablespoon each of burnt salt and corn meal.

SODA LOTION FOR BURNS.

Mix the soda in water, with or without camphor. Keep a soft rag wet with it on the burned place.

TO REMOVE FRECKLES.

Alum and lemon juice, one ounce of each, mixed with one pint rose-water. Apply three times a day with a sponge. It will remove freckles, blotches and pimples.

TO RENEW LARD.

Heat the lard and throw in sliced raw potatoes.

FOR CHAPPED HANDS.

Camphor and glycerine, in equal parts.

Soiled clothes may be put in hot soap-suds, but never in hot clear water.

BAKING-POWDER.
Mrs. Clough.

Six ounces tartaric acid, eight ounces best soda, one quart flour. Mix through a sieve.

SOFT SOAP.
Mrs. Bugbee.

Take two pounds of potash, add three gallons soft water. Stir and boil until all is dissolved. Then add five pounds of any kind of refuse grease. Boil until well mixed. Let stand until nearly cold, and add sufficient warm water to make it the required thickness.

COUGH DROPS.
Mrs. Weyer.

One handful each of hoarhound, hops and mullen. Simmer in one quart water, strain, and to the tea add two pounds brown sugar, four lemons and twenty-five cents' worth gumarabic. Boil until a thick syrup.

TO MAKE GOOD VINEGAR IN THREE WEEKS.
Mrs. Bugbee.

One quart molasses, one pint yeast, three gallons warm rain water. Put all into a jug, and tie a piece of gauze over the bung to keep out flies and yet admit the air. In hot weather set it in the sun, in cold weather set it by the stove, and in three weeks you will have good vinegar.

TABLE OF MEASURES.

Wheat flour, one pound is one quart.
Corn meal, one pound and two ounces is one quart.
Butter, soft, one pound is one quart.
Loaf sugar, broken, one pound is one quart.
Sugar, pounded, one pound and one ounce is one quart.
Sixteen large teaspoonsful are one-half pint.
Eight large teaspoonsful are one gill.
Four large teaspoonsful are one-half gill.
Two gills are one-half pint.
Two pints are one quart.
Four quarts are one gallon.
A common-sized tumbler holds one-half pint.
Ten eggs are one pound.
A teacup holds one gill.
A tablespoon is one-half ounce.
One teaspoonful is sixty drops.
Two cups are one pint.
Ten pounds fine XXX chain makes twenty-eight yards rag carpet. One pound and one-half woolen rags to one yard; one and one-fourth pounds cotton rags to one yard.

WEDDINGS.

Mrs. Arndt.

One year, cotton; two years, straw; three years, paper; four years, leather; five years, wooden; seven years, iron; eight years, woolen; ten years, tin; twelve years, linen; fifteen years, glass; eighteen years, silk; twenty years, china; twenty-five years, silver; thirty years, pearl; forty years, ruby or gem; fifty years, golden; seventy-five years, diamond.

TO PRESERVE EGGS FOR WINTER USE.
Mrs. Bugbee.

For every three gallons of water, put in one pint of fresh slacked lime, and one-half pint of common salt; mix well. Put in the eggs carefully so as not to break the shell. Keep the eggs covered with the brine, and this will not fail you.

CURE FOR BOILS.

Make a boiled paste of fine flour stiff enough to allow a spoon to stand up in it; take it off the fire; add a full teaspoon of butter and two of soft soap to every cup of paste.

BURN SALVE.

Two ounces Burgundy pitch, half an ounce of beeswax, two tablespoons of lard melted together. Soften by heating when used, and spread on linen cloth, or kid.

CURE FOR A CANCER.

Stir the yelk of an egg with salt until a salve is formed; put it on a piece of sticking-plaster and apply twice a day. One-fourth of an ounce of carbolic acid in one quart water makes a good wash for a cancer.

A SURE PREVENTIVE OF, OR CURE FOR CHAPPED HANDS.
Miss Mamie Sappington, Madison, Ind.

The juice of one lemon to same amount of glycerine. Apply, after washing the hands, and wipe dry.

TO TAKE PAINT FROM WINDOW GLASS.

Rub it off with a copper cent.

TO TAKE OIL FROM CARPET.

Rub the spot over with hard soap after putting the soap in water; then rub off the soap with a cloth dipped in ammonia and water.

TO POLISH NICKLE-PLATE STOVES.

Mix Spanish whiting with ammonia and water; rub off with flannel.

TO BLACK A STOVE.

Mix benzine, black lead and varnish into a thin paste.

TO CLEAN WINDOW GLASS.

Cover with dampened Spanish whiting, and when almost dry, rub off with dry flannel. A very little washing soda in warm water cleans glass easily.

TO PRESERVE STOVE-PIPES.

Wash them, while warm, with linseed oil before putting them away in the spring.

FOR CLEANING HAIR BRUSHES.

Take corn meal and fill the brush; rub gently with the hand; as it absorbs the grease, shake it out and use fresh, until the brush is clean.

VARNISH FOR GRATES.

Asphaltum dissolved in turpentine.

FURNITURE POLISH.
Mrs. Fletcher Rubush.

Five ounces linseed oil, two ounces turpentine, and one-half ounce oil of vitrol. Coal oil may be rubbed over furniture, and give a temporary polish.

COUGH SYRUP.
Mrs. Kerper.

Virginia snake-root, five cents; elecampane, five cents; spikenard, five cents; cumfrey, five cents; liquorice, five cents; wild cherry bark, five cents. Moisten with boiling water; boil with sugar to make a syrup.

SALTS OF LEMON.

Equal parts of oxalic and tartaric acid. It will remove iron rust or ink stains.

ERASIVE COMPOUND.

Boil one ounce of castile soap in water until it is dissolved; powder, and add two ounces washing or sal-soda, one-half ounce starch, one-fourth ounce borax, and one pint water. When dissolved, pour into cups or boxes.

SMELLING SALTS.

To one pint of ammonia add one drachm of ottar of rosemary, one drachm of English lavender, one-half drachm bergamot, and one-fourth drachm of cloves.

COLD CREAM.

Four ounces oil of Almonds, two drachms white wax, same of spermaceti. Melt and add four ounces rose-water and one ounce orange-water.

FOR FROSTED FEET.

Ten cents' worth of oil of organum.

FOR SORE MOUTH.

Powdered tannin or powdered yellow-root.

FOR CHAPPED LIPS.

Vasaline or glycerine.

GOOD TONIC.

TIMBERLAKE, Druggist.

℞ Fluid extract sarsaparilla.................ʒii
    Fluid extract dandelion..................ʒi
    Syrup stillingia co......................ʒi
    Iodide potash..........................ʒii
    Syrup Simplex..........................ʒi
    Aq. fontana...........................ʒii

Take one tablespoonful three times a day.

COUGH MIXTURE.

Mrs. Kerper.

Gumarabic, pulverized, three cents; liquorice, three cents; ipecac, three cents; laudanum, three cents; paregoric, six cents; hive syrup, six cents. Add one cup molasses and one cup vinegar; mix cold; take a tablespoonful three times a day.

REMEDY FOR SORE THROAT.

Timberlake, Druggist.

℞ Tincture iron............................℥ii
   Chlorate potash.........................℥ii
   Syrup simple and aq. font., of each..........℥ii

Mix. Take a teaspoonful in a little water, and gargle; swallow a little if necessary.

MUSTARD PLASTER.

One tablespoon molasses stirred thick with mustard; spread on a cloth and apply. It will not blister for more than an hour. If desired to irritate, mix with water or vinegar; spread on a very thin cloth.

HOP POULTICE.

Boil a half teacup of hops in a pint of water; put in a bag, or mix with corn meal and spread on a cloth.

BREAD POULTICE.

Crumble stale bread; boil until soft, and spread on a cloth.

SLIPPERY-ELM POULTICE.

Stir pulverized slippery-elm bark into hot milk and water. This poultice removes inflammation.

EMETIC.

One-half glass warm water, one teaspoon salt, and one teaspoon mustard.

TO STOP NOSE-BLEEDING.

Put a key, or a cold, wet towel down the back between the shoulders; or raise the arms above the head; or, if possible, obtain from the drug store Monsel's Powder. This powder stops the bleeding of any artery.

ANTIDOTES.

If poison has been taken, induce vomiting by using salt and mustard in cold water; a cup of strong coffee, and then the whites of two eggs, may be given in haste, but it is best to send for a physician.

TO PREVENT HYDROPHOBIA.

Rub nitrate of silver in the wound.

COUNTRY SOAP.
Mrs. S. E. Wagoner.

Incline the platform on which the ash-barrel stands; put straw in the bottom of the barrel; pour in hard-wood ashes; dampen them; when the barrel is nearly full, pour on boiling water until the lye begins to drip, and then pour in cold water; fill a large, iron kettle with this lye; let it be strong enough to strip a feather; then add ham rinds, drippings from frying-pans, and other refuse grease, as long as the lye will absorb it; boil until thick.

FLOUR STARCH, OR PASTE.

One quart boiling water, three tablespoonsful of flour smoothed in cold water. Pour in and stir until it boils; for paste it should be thicker; strain through a crash towel.

TO MEND COAL-BUCKETS.
Mrs. Merrill,

Paste a cloth on the outside and one on the inside of the hole; make a mortar of one cup coarse salt and two cups wood-ashes; put it on inside of bucket one-half inch thick, and let it harden.

SUGGESTIONS.

To blanche almonds: Pour boiling water on them to take off the brown skin.

To candy orange peel: Make a thin syrup of loaf sugar and water; put in the strips of peeling and boil one-half hour; then put the pieces into a thick syrup and boil until the sugar clings to them; take them out, drain and dry.

To use baking-powder: Always sift it in the flour; cream tartar should also be in the flour, and soda used with it should be in the sweet milk; soda used with sour milk should be put in the milk to effervesce.

To prevent juice from soaking into pie-crust, wet the crust with the white of an egg.

Pie crust, or pastry: Puff-paste is one pound of flour and one pound of lard and butter crumbled together and wet slightly with cold water; a plainer crust can be made with less shortening.

A little lump of baking soda tenders roast beef when put in the pan. It also improves many vegetables, especially if the water is hard.

Stock for soup can be kept by constantly saving from the meat platter, and also by cutting the bones out before broiling the beef steaks. Boiling these fragments furnishes a good foundation for soup.

It is important to systematize the work of the house.

Washing should be done on Monday.

Ironing should be done on Tuesday.

Bread baking and kitchen cleaning, on Wednesday.

Sewing and visiting, on Thursday.

Sweeping and dusting, on Friday.

Bread and cake baking, on Saturday.

ADDITIONAL RECIPES.

CALF-HEAD SOUP.
Mrs. Irwin Harrison.

Put the head in strong salt-water for one hour, to draw out the blood; take out the brains carefully and put them on to boil; put the head in as much water as you want soup; add a large spoonful of salt; when tender, cut the head into small pieces and put back into the pot, with one onion finely chopped; add one teaspoon sweet marjorum, one of sweet basil, one of summer savory, one of allspice, and one-fourth teaspoon cayenne; add more salt and let boil several hours; one hour before the soup is done mash the brains with the yelks of three hard-boiled eggs, a large cup catsup, and one-half pint browned flour; thin this with cold water and pour in the soup, stirring frequently; make little dumplings or force meat balls; when dished, add a slice of lemon to the soup.

BEEF SOUP.
Mrs. J. R. Nichols.

The stock for beef soup should be prepared the day before you wish to use it. To do this take a shin bone, put it in a large earthen vessel or porcelain-lined kettle nearly full of cold water. Cover closely; set on top of stove, and boil slowly four or five hours, until the meat is in shreds and all the marrow is cleaned out of the bone, which should have been cracked well before boiling. Set away the vessel in a cool place until the next day. Skim off the cake of tallow from the top; lift out all the bones and shreds of meat with a perforated ladle. You now have the foundation for any kind of beef soup. Just as good stock can be made with the bones cut out of your beef steaks saved up for a few days.

CLEAR VEGETABLE SOUP.
Mrs. Will Gregg, Hillsboro, Ohio.

About an hour before dinner, set your vessel with your prepared stock on the stove. In a separate vessel cook in as little water as possible, three or four potatoes sliced, a turnip, an onion shredded, some cabbage, also shredded; a few tomatoes and a sliced carrot. When the vegetables are tender, turn them into the boiling stock; cook all about twenty minutes, season and strain through a colander into the tureen. The potatoes must not be cooked to a mush or they will cloud the soup. Pick out a few slices of carrot and put them in the tureen.

MILK SOUP.
Mrs. Robert Rhodes, Kansas City.

After your stock becomes hot add a pint of milk, rub together a tablespoonful of butter and three tablespoonsful of flour, adding a little milk to work it smooth, thicken the broth with this, boiling it fifteen or twenty minutes, season to taste. Have ready an egg beaten in a little milk or water, stir it into the soup after you have removed it from over the fire. Eat with crackers like oyster soup, or pour over squares of bread fried brown. To make noodle or macaroni soup of this, put the noodles into the soup and boil twenty minutes, and after swelling the macaroni in a separate vessel, add it to the soup, and boil ten or fifteen minutes.

FOR CURING MEAT.
Mrs. Enos, Sr.

Six gallons water, nine pounds salt, coarse and fine mixed, three pounds sugar, three ounces saltpeter, one ounce pearl ash, one quart molasses. Boil, and skim these ingredients well, and when cold, pour it over the beef or pork.

TO MAKE STEAK TENDER.
Mrs. Hereth.

Put three tablespoons salad oil and one tablespoon vinegar well mixed together, on a large flat dish. Lay the steak on this dressing; after one-half hour turn it on the other side. Salt must not be put on.

VEAL LOAF.
Mrs. Coburn.

Three pounds veal chopped fine, three-fourths pound pickled-pork chopped fine, twelve crackers rolled and sifted, pepper, salt and butter to season. Bake one hour.

WASHINGTON CHOW-CHOW.
Mrs. Baggs.

One and one-half pecks green tomatoes, two large heads cabbage, fifteen large onions, twenty-five cucumbers, one pint grated horseradish, one-half pound Welsh mustard seed, one ounce celery seed, one-half pint small onions (not cut), one-half teacup each ground pepper, tumeric and cinnamon. Chop the tomatoes, cabbage, cucumbers and large onions in pieces and pack in salt over night; drain well and mix in the spices; boil one and one-half gallons good vinegar and pour over boiling hot; boil over the same vinegar three mornings and pour over hot; the third morning add vinegar, two boxes mustard, one-half pint sweet oil, and one pound brown sugar.

MANGOES.
Mrs. S. M. Sappington, Madison, Ind.

Having cut them and taken out the seeds, put them in a jar with one pint salt, and cover with boiling water; next morning wipe them; make a filling of red cabbage, onions, horseradish, salt, ground black pepper, and white mustard seed; fill and sew up; pour over boiling hot vinegar.

SWEET PICKLES.
Mrs. Frank Martin.

Ten pounds fruit, five pounds sugar, one quart good vinegar, cloves and cinnamon to suit taste. Boil sugar and vinegar together; skim, and put in the fruit; cook done, take out, boil the syrup down and pour over the fruit; tie the spices in a cloth and boil in the syrup.

CHINESE PICKLES.
Mrs. Branham.

Two dozen green tomatoes, two dozen large green cucumbers, peeled; six large green peppers, one dozen onions, six heads celery, one head cabbage. Chop all fine, put in a jar, stir in a teacup of salt, let it stand over night, then drain in a colander. Boil in two quarts of vinegar and two quarts of water; drain and put in a jar. Put in kettle on the stove, one gallon vinegar, two pounds brown sugar, one cup mustard seed, three tablespoons ground mustard, one tablespoon mace, three tablespoons cloves, one tablespoon cayenne pepper, one tablespoon allspice, and one ounce coriander seed; scald and pour over the pickles in jar; cover close.

CURRY POWDER FOR GRAVIES.
Mrs. Mary E. Lilly.

One ounce ginger, one ounce mustard, one ounce black pepper, three ounces coriander seed, three ounces tumeric, one-fourth ounce cayenne pepper, one-half ounce cardamon seed, one-half ounce curnion seed, one-half ounce cinnamon. Pound very fine and cork tight.

NEW ENGLAND BROWN BREAD.
Mrs. C. J. Parker.

Four cups corn meal, two cups rye meal, four cups sweet milk, two cups sour milk, two cups molasses, one teaspoon soda. Steam until done, and then put in oven until it forms a light-brown crust.

GRAHAM AND INDIAN BROWN BREAD.
Mrs. Myron W. Reed.

Three cups corn meal, two cups Graham flour, one pint milk, three-fourths cup molasses, one teaspoon saleratus.

Pour into a two-quart pan and steam for three hours; set in the oven for twenty minutes, or until a thick crust forms; eat warm.

SANDWICHES.
Mrs. Forgus.

Sardines chopped fine, a little chopped ham, also chopped pickles. Mix with mustard, pepper, salt and vinegar.

POTATO SALAD.
Mrs. Cady.

Four potatoes boiled, peeled and sliced; one-half small onion cut fine; two small bunches celery chopped fine; whites of two hard-boiled eggs. Mix with oil, mustard, pepper, salt and vinegar, to taste.

SPICED PLUMS.
Mrs. Noel.

One gallon plums, one pint vinegar, one quart sugar, cinnamon and cloves, whole. Boil several hours and seal tight.

PLUM PUDDING.
Mrs. Mary Ayres, Houston, Texas.

One quart flour, one pint milk, six ounces suet, six ounces sugar, one-half pound raisins, one teaspoon soda, one-half teaspoon salt. Boil in a mold; eat with sauce.

FIG PUDDING.
Mrs. Addie C. Forgus.

One cup bread crumbs, one cup suet, one cup milk, one cup sugar, one-half pound figs, one teaspoon baking-powder; chop suet and figs together. Steam two hours.

DELICIOUS PUDDING.
Mrs. Forgus.

Yelks of three eggs, white of one egg, two ounces each powdered sugar, butter and flour; beat smooth. Add one-half pint milk. Bake in pie pans twenty minutes. Place one on top of the other, and eat with sauce.

LACEY'S

⇢FINE⇠

Photographs,

ALL MADE BY THE

"Instantaneous Process."

VANCE BLOCK,

Cor. Virginia Ave. and Washington Street.

ENTRANCE ELEVATOR.

J. A. LYONS,

WHOLESALE AND RETAIL DEALER IN

STOVES, TINWARE

And General House Furnishing Goods.

Practical Tin, Copper and Sheet Iron Worker.

ALSO, AGENT FOR THE
MICHIGAN STOVE CO. and the celebrated "GARLAND."

Roofing and Repairing Neatly and Promptly Done.

86 & 88 S. Delaware St. and 88 W. Washington St.,

INDIANAPOLIS, IND.

Kingan & Co. (L'td.)

PORK PACKERS AND CURERS

OF THE "**RELIABLE**" BRAND OF SUGAR CURED MEATS.

MEAT MARKET:

WEST END MARYLAND STREET.

Fresh Beef and Pork of Choice Quality.
Kettle Rendered Lard for Family Use.

A. TIMBERLAKE,
Druggist and Apothecary,

Fine Toilet Soaps, Brushes, Combs, etc.

PERFUMERY AND FANCY TOILET ARTICLES, SCHOOL BOOKS, STATIONERY, ETC.

Besides, every other article of the best quality, usually kept by a store-keeper.

N. W. Cor. College Ave. and Seventh St.

P. S.—iF YoU geT Sick In tHe NiGht, coMe oVeR, I'm HerE.

CAPITAL
BAKING POWDER,

ABSOLUTELY PURE.

Never fails to make the most delicious biscuit and pastry.

MANUFACTURED BY

F. JENNINGS,

For Sale by all Dealers.   **INDIANAPOLIS, IND.**

JOSEPH BECKER,
"The Confectioner,"

KEEPS CONSTANTLY AT HIS RESTAURANT,

20 W. Washington St.,

Standard Ice Cream and **Milk Bread, Home-made.**

WEDDINGS AND PARTIES FURNISHED ENTIRE A SPECIALTY.

INDIANAPOLIS, - - - INDIANA.

Chartered 1851. Amended 1875.

INDIANA
Insurance Company,

Nos. 62 and 64 EAST MARKET STREET,
INDIANAPOLIS, IND.

Fire Insurance, Stock Company.

N. S. BYRAM, Pres't. M. V. McGILLIARD, Sec'y.
CHAS. E. DARK, Treas. E. G. CORNELIUS, Vice-Pres't.

Directors:

HON. VINSON CARTER, Attorney at Law.
CHAS E. DARK, Teller at Indiana Banking Company.
R. H. McCREA, of Fahnley & McCrea, Wholesale Millinery.
ELI LILLY, Manufacturing Pharmacist.
FRANCIS A. COFFIN, Sec'y and Treas. Indianapolis Cabinet Co.
M. V. McGILLIARD, Insurance Agent.

M. V. McGILLIARD,

General Insurance Agent,

—

Large Lines of Insurance placed promptly anywhere in Indiana.

Represents leading American and Foreign Co's.

Call and see us or correspond with us, at

62 & 64 East Market Street,

INDIANAPOLIS, IND.

FLOATING ISLAND.
Mrs. Charlie McMullin.

One quart milk, four eggs beaten separately. Stir until it boils. Remove, and flavor with lemon. Spread over the hot custard, the beaten whites of the four eggs, and grate loaf-sugar and cocoanut on the top. Serve cold.

SUET PUDDING.
Mrs. Mary Kingston.

One cup chopped suet, three eggs, one cup sweet milk, one cup raisins, two cups flour, two teaspoons baking-powder, spices, and a pinch of salt. Flour the suet and raisins before adding to the batter; boil two hours; serve with a sauce made of butter and sugar beaten to a cream, and the beaten white of one egg; flavor to taste.

CURRANT PUDDING.
Mrs. John Hart.

One cup sugar, two eggs, one lump butter size of an egg, one cup water, flour to make stiff batter, two teaspoons baking-powder; mix in one cup dried currants.

STEAMED FRUIT PUDDING.
Mrs. Haughey.

Make a batter of two cups sweet milk, two tablespoons butter, two eggs, and three cups of flour; add three teaspoons baking-powder. Butter some cups, set them in a steamer over boiling water. Drop in a little batter and some berries until the cups are two-thirds full. Put the cover on the steamer and steam thirty minutes. Eat with cream and sugar.

SCOTCH PIE.
Mrs. Kerper.

Mince enough ripe apples to fill a deep dish; then make a stiff batter of one pint sweet milk, one tablespoon melted butter, two teaspoons baking-powder in almost one quart of flour. With a knife, spread the batter over the apples. When either baked or steamed, turn upside down on a plate and season with butter and sugar.

ORANGE PIE.
Mrs. Gates.

Juice and part of the rind of one orange, two tablespoons corn-starch, one teacup hot water with one-fourth box of gelatine dissolved in it. Mix and bake. This is for two pies.

VINEGAR PIE.
Mrs. Jane Mead, Minneapolis, Minn.

One cup sugar, one-half cup vinegar. Boil together and cool. Add one tablespoon flour, one egg, one rolled cracker, one teaspoon butter. Make two crusts.

MOCK MINCE PIE.
Mrs. Lizzie Irvin.

One cup each of sugar, molasses and water; one-fourth cup butter, one-half cup vinegar, three slices of wheat bread crumbled, raisins and spices. Make with two crusts.

APPLE PIE.
Miss Rena Newton.

Pare and cut in half, four or five apples; make a rich crust, placing the apples in, and then putting on sugar, butter, cinnamon and cream, no upper crust being used.

CREAM PIE.
Mrs. Jennie Caldwell.

Make a rich under crust, and bake until almost done; then put in the custard already prepared, using two eggs, one tablespoon corn-starch, sugar and flavoring to taste; add milk to nearly fill the pie-pan.

APPLE MERINGUE.
Mrs. J. H. Shreve.
Line a deep baking-pan with pie-crust; put in a layer of stewed apples; next a layer of thin-sliced bread buttered on both sides; next another layer of apples. Bake, and when done take the whites of two eggs beaten to a stiff froth and spread over the top; put in the oven and brown.

CREAM PIE.
Mrs. Morse.
One and one-half cups milk, yelks of two eggs, two tablespoons sugar, one heaping table-spoon corn-starch, one-half of lemon peel grated. Beat well together and cook as for custard; make pastry as for any pie and bake; turn the boiled custard into the crust; then take the whites of the eggs, beaten to a stiff froth with one heaping tablespoon sugar; spread over the top of the pie; set in the oven and brown.

TRANSPARENT PIE.
Mrs. Maggie Gregg, Hillsboro, Ohio.
One cup butter, one cup powdered white sugar, four eggs well beaten. Bake the crust and pour in the mixture; put back in the oven until the custard stiffens.

ITALIAN CREAM.
Mrs. Noel.
One quart milk, three eggs, six tablepoons sugar, three tablespoons corn starch. Boil like custard. Make a meringue of the whites and a little sugar; add vanilla.

LEMON SPONGE.
One-half box Cox's gelatine dissolved over the fire in one and one-half pints water. Add one pound white sugar and the grated rinds of two lemons, with the juice of three lemons. Boil a few moments, and when nearly cold add the whites of three eggs beaten stiff. Beat well together, and especially as it thickens. Pour into molds and serve with cream.

LEMON BUTTER.
Mrs. Wilson.

Three grated lemons, three beaten eggs, and one pint sugar; add butter the size of an egg. Boil until it thickens.

PRESERVED ORANGES.
Mrs. B. W. Thomas.

Boil in soft water until you can run a straw through the skin. To three-fourths of a pound of sugar, add one pound of fruit. Take the oranges from the water and pour the hot syrup over them. Let them stand until next day, and boil them in the syrup until it is thick. Take them out and strain the syrup over them.

GUAVA JELLY.
Mrs. Gates.

Slice the guavas and cover them with water; cook until done, and strain; add one pint of sugar to one pint of juice, and cook until it is jelly.

PRESERVED CITRON.
Mrs. T. H. K. Enos.

Pare the melons, take out the seeds, and cut in squares half an inch thick. Lay in salt and water one hour. Wash off and boil in strong ginger tea. Make a weak syrup of sugar and water. Boil ten minutes, and then make a syrup of one pound of sugar to one pound of citron. Boil in this until it looks clear, and season with lemon peel.

ORANGE OR LEMON MARMALADE.
Mrs. Lina Graydon.

Twelve pounds rather sour oranges, or twelve pounds of lemons. For the oranges, use twelve pounds of sugar; for the lemons, use eighteen pounds of sugar. Pare the fruit, cover the parings twice their depth with water. Boil until tender, then drain. Halve the fruit crosswise, press out the juice and soft pulp. Cover the white skins with three quarts cold water, and boil one-half hour. Strain the water in the orange juice, cut the rinds into shreds, add them to the juice and boil ten minutes; add the sugar and boil down.

GINGER CRACKERS.
Miss M. E. Knerr.

One quart New Orleans molasses, one-half pound butter and lard, one-half pound brown sugar, one tablespoon each of ginger and cinnamon. Add flour to stiffen, and roll out.

HICKORYNUT MACARONI.
Miss M. E. Knerr.

The whites of five eggs, one pound granulated sugar, one tablespoon flour, one pound chopped nut kernels. Beat the eggs to a froth; drop on tins.

DROP CAKE.
Miss Mary E. Knerr.

One pound sugar, one-half pound butter, one pound flour, one pound currants, four eggs, and flavoring.

BAKER'S POUND CAKE.
Mrs. Kerper.

Two cups sugar, three-fourths cup butter, three eggs, one cup milk, three cups flour, two teaspoons baking-powder. Add nutmeg.

TEA CAKE.
Mrs. Myron W. Reed.

One cup sugar, heaping tablespoon butter, three-fourths cup milk, one egg, two cups flour, two even teaspoonsful baking-powder. Bake in a shallow pan; is nice warm for tea. Warranted good.

DOLLY-VARDEN CAKE.
Mrs. Marx E. Lilly.

Dark Part—One cup sugar, one-half cup butter, one-half cup molasses, two-thirds cup milk, two cups flour, one egg and the yelks of four eggs, two teaspoons baking-powder in the flour, one teaspoon cloves, two teaspoons cinnamon, one-half nutmeg grated, one and one-half cups chopped raisins, and one-half cup figs in the icing between the layers of cake.

Light Part—One pound flour, one pound sugar, one-half pound butter, one teacup milk, six eggs beaten separately, three teaspoons baking-powder, grated rind and juice of one lemon.

ICING:

One-half teacup water, three teacups sugar, whites of three eggs. Boil water and sugar until thick; pour over the beaten whites, and beat until cool.

TO ICE A CAKE.
Mrs. Jerre Black, Hillsboro, Ohio.

Break the whites of four eggs into a flat dish with one handful powdered sugar; beat it well with a silver fork for five minutes; then add more sugar until one pound is used; keep whipping until the icing is fine and firm; if lemon juice is used as flavoring, use more sugar; pour on the center of the cake and spread smoothly with a broad-bladed knife dipped in cold water.

DATE CAKE.
Mrs. Ira Bugbee.

One cup butter, two cups granulated sugar, one cup milk, four cups flour, four eggs, one-half cup nutmeg grated, one-half teaspoon ground mace, grated rind of one lemon, one pound dates stoned and chopped and rubbed in flour, three teaspoons baking-powder.

CITRON CAKE.
Mrs. Rufus D. Black.

Two cups butter, two cups sugar, one pound citron, four and one-half cups flour, whites of twelve eggs, one-half cup milk, and three teaspoons baking-powder.

MARBLE CAKE.
Mrs. Wm. H. Webb.

Two cups sugar, one cup butter, whites of eight eggs beaten to a stiff froth, three cups flour, with two teaspoons baking-powder.

Dark Part—One and one-half cups brown sugar, three-fourths cup butter, two and one-half cups flour, two teaspoons baking-powder, one tablespoon each of cinnamon, allspice and cloves. Add one grated nutmeg, and pepper.

AMBROSIA CAKE.
Mrs. David Reynolds.

One-half cup milk, three-fourths cup butter, two cups sugar, three cups flour, four eggs, three teaspoons baking-powder. Bake in layers.

FILLING:

One pint whipped cream, one grated cocoanut, two eggs, one cup sugar, two oranges, and the grated rind of one orange.

IMPERIAL CAKE.
Mrs. Paul Hereth.

One pound sugar, one pound butter, one pound flour, three-fourths pound citron, one pound raisins, one pound blanched and cut almonds, ten eggs, one cup currants, one grated nutmeg. Bake one and one-half hours.

KITCHEN UTENSILS.

Kitchen table.	Wash-bench.
Water-buckets.	Three tubs.
Wash-board.	Range or cooking stove.
Gas, gasoline, or oil stove.	Two frying-pans.
Two griddles.	Tea-kettle.
Sauce-pans.	Steamer.
Good granite-ware kettles, two sizes.	Bread-pans.
	Cake-pans.
Gem-pans.	One quart-measure.

KITCHEN UTENSILS—Continued.

Scales and weights.
Cake-turner.
Iron spoons.
Tea-caddy.
Wooden sugar-bucket.
Dish-pans.
Pie-pans.
Potato-masher.
Grater.
Hammer.
Waffle-irons.
Dish-mop.
Brooms.
Perforated ladle.
Bread-board.
Tin bread-box.
Tin cake-box.
Towel-roller.
Clothes-stick.
Clothes-pins.
Clothes-wringer.
Clothes-basket.
Ironing-board.
Fluting-iron.
Step-ladder.
Roller-towels.
Steel knives and forks.
Toasting-rack.
Boiler.
Baking-dishes.
Lantern.
Clock.
Ash-bucket.
Crumb-brush and pan.
One pint-measure.
Dippers.
Coffee-mill.
Coffee-pot.
Coffee-can.
Jelly-cake pans.
Flour sieve.
Funnels.
Flat-irons.
Can-opener.
Spice-box.
Floor-mop.
Chopping-bowl.
Shallow, tin skimmer.
Rolling-pin.
Meat-knife.
Meat-saw.
Flat-iron stand.
Market-basket.
Starch-box.
Salt-box.
Pepper-box.
Bosom-board.
Dust-pans.
Dish-towels.
Sausage-grinder.
Ice-pick.
Grid-iron.
Stoneware crocks.
Stone fruit-bowls.
Match-box.
Matches.
Wood-box or coal-bucket.

CONTENTS.

PAGE.

BUTTER.

Butter 1-3

BREAD, ETC.

Stock Yeast, Self-Working Yeast, Potato Yeast, Dry Yeast, Salt-Rising Bread, Sour Milk Bread, Sweet Milk Bread, Buttermilk Bread, Hominy Bread, Rice Bread, Rye Bread, Graham Bread, Yankee Bread, Quick Brown Bread, Steamed Brown Bread Compressed Yeast Bread, Light Rolls, Ordinary Rolls, Superior Rolls, Steamboat Rolls, Imperial Rolls, English Rolls, French Rolls, German Rolls, Graham Rolls, Parker-House Rolls, Pocket-Book Rolls, Egg Rolls, Sally Lunn, Risen Sally Lunn, Baking-Powder Sally Lunn, Rusk, Wafers, Crumpets, Buttermilk Muffins, Baking-Powder Muffins, Yeast Muffins, Mixed Muffins, Cinnamon Muffins, Graham Muffins, Rice Muffins, Graham Gems, Minnesota Gems, Rice Corn Bread, Steamed Corn Bread, Risen Corn Bread, Corn Pone, Corn Dodgers, Corn Johnny-Cake, Sour Milk Waffles, Baking-Powder Waffles, Rice Waffles, Rice Croquetts, Buns, Puffs, Batter-Cakes, Eggless Batter-Cakes, Graham Flour Batter-Cakes, Buckwheat Batter-Cakes, Corn Batter-Cakes, Rice Batter-Cakes, Bread Batter-Cakes, Bannocks, Vanities, Oat Meal Fritters, Hominy Fritters, Corn Meal Mush Fritters, Parsnip Fritters, Squash Fritters, Snow Fritters, Cucumber Fritters, Apple Fritters, Clam Fritters, Oyster Fritters, Rice Fritters, Ripe Tomato Fritters, Green Tomato Fritters, Corn Fritters, Baking-Powder Biscuit, Soda Biscuit, Vienna Biscuit, Buttermilk Biscuit, Beat Biscuit, Kentucky Beat Biscuit, Cracker Toast, To Freshen Crackers, Biscuit and Rolls...... 3-28

Additional Bread Recipes................................... 180

SOUPS.

PAGE.

Celery Soup, Beef Soup, Veal Soup, Mutton Soup, Oyster Soup, Noodle Soup, Potato Soup, Corn Soup, Bean Soup, Pea Soup, Tomato Soup, Tit-Bit Soup...................................... 28–30
Additional Soup Recipes................................... 172–173

FISH.

Baked Fish, Boiled Fish, Halibut, Lobster, Mackerel, Cod Fish, Salmon, Egg Sauce For Fish, Mayonaise Dressing......... 31–33

OYSTERS.

Fried Oysters, Stewed Oysters, Escalloped Oysters, Pickled Oysters, Macaroni and Oysters, Sweet Breads and Oysters, Oyster Pie, Oyster Salad.. 33–34

MEATS, ETC.

Mock Duck, Ham Toast, Lamb Steaks, Pork Fritters, Pressed Beef, Pressed Chicken, Boiled Ham, Smothered Spring Chicken, Chicken Pie, Roast Veal, Roast Beef, Veal Loaf, Meat Puffs, For Curing Meat, Veal Stew, Lard, Sausage, Scrapple, Croquetts, Beef Hash, Corn-Beef Hash, Corn-Beef Liver, Broiled Beefsteak, Fried Beefsteak, Veal Marble, Italian Cheese, Sandwiches, To Roast Fowls, Turkey Dressing, Tongue 35–43

EGGS.

Boiled Eggs, Poached Eggs, Scrambled Eggs, Omelette, Potatoes with Omelette, Stuffed Omelette, Egg Balls............43-44

VEGETABLES.

Escalloped Tomatoes, Fried Tomatoes, Broiled Tomatoes, Stewed Tomatoes, Baked Tomatoes, Sliced Tomatoes, Corn and Tomatoes, Stewed Corn, Fried Corn, Corn Pudding, Succotash, Lima Beans, String Beans, Baked Beans, Boston Baked Beans, Yankee Baked Beans, Canning Corn, Green Peas, Cauliflower, Spinach, Potato Croquetts, Potatoes and Cauliflower, Sweet Potatoes, Potatoes and Turnips, Egg-Plant, Squash, Corn Oysters, Mushrooms, Salsify or Oyster-Plant, Asparagus, Macaroni, Kalekannon, Ochra, Beets, Smothered Potatoes, Potato Puffs, Rules for Cooking Vegetables........45-52

SALADS.

Slaw, Onion Slaw, Potato Salad, Chicken or Turkey Salad, Veal Salad, Lettuce Salad, Egg Salad, Lobster Salad, White Fish or Trout Salad, Tomato Salad, Sweet-Bread Salad, Oyster Salad, Celery Salad, Raw Catsup, Currant Catsup, Tomato Catsup, Oil Pickles, Cucumber Soy, Green Tomato Soy.....53-57

PICKLES.

PAGE.

Mixed Pickles, Green Tomato Pickles, Artichoke Pickles, Bean Pickles, Mango Pickles, Chow-Chow, Pickled Oysters, Pickled Cucumbers, Pickled Walnuts, Pickled Onions, Pickled Eggs, Cucumber Catsup, Walnut Catsup, Tomato Catsup, Chili Sauce, Cold Slaw, Hot Slaw, Celery Slaw, Tomato Slaw, Chopped Pickles, Sliced Tomato Pickles, Sliced Cucumber Pickles...58–64

Additional Pickle Recipes.............................174–175

PIES.

Vinegar Pie, Green Apple Pie, Cream Apple Pie, Tomato Pie, Lemon Pie, Cocoanut Pie, Chess Pie, Mock Mince Pie, Dried Apple Pie, Blackberry Pie, Plum Pie, Tennessee Sweet Potato Pie, Aunt Charlotte Pie, Custard Pie, Jelly Pie, Pumpkin Pie, Lemon Custard Pie, Potatoe Custard Pie, Mince Pie, Layer Pie, German Puffs, Strawberry Shortcake................65–73

Additional Pie Recipes................................177–179

PUDDINGS.

Citron Pudding, Lemon Pudding, Fig Pudding, Cake Pudding, Quick Pudding, Cabinet Pudding, Cocoanut Pudding, French Pudding, Rice Pudding, Baked Roll Pudding, Farmer's Apple Pudding, Charlotte Russe, Cream Whips, Steamed Roly-Poly, Apple Meringue, Charleston Pudding, Cottage Pudding, Sliced Bread Pudding, Tapioca Pudding, Snow Pudding, Apple Pudding, Plum Pudding, Batter Pudding, Blackberry Slump, Corn-Starch Pudding, Cream Pudding, Gelatine Pudding, Orange Souffle, Orange Pudding, Queen of Puddings, Arrowroot Pudding, Butter Roll, Bird's Nest Sago Pudding, Strawberry Pudding, Steamed Pudding, Sweet Potato Pudding, Cranberry Pudding, Banana Cream, Gelatine Blanc-Mange, Angel Food, Sago Pudding, Bread Pudding, Fifteen-Minute Pudding....74–89

Additional Pudding Recipes...........................176–177

CAKE.

Fruit Cake, Pork Cake, Scotch Cake, Velvet Cake, Fancy Pound Cake, Confectioner's Cake, Cup Cake, Corn-Starch Cake, Sponge Cake, Chocolate-Icing Cake, One-Egg Cake, White Sponge Cake, Pink Marble Cake, White Cake, Jam Cake, Spiced Cake, Hickorynut Cake, Chocolate Cake, Chocolate Marble Cake, Eggless Cake, Lady Cake, Orange Cake, Home Fruit Cake, Cocoanut Loaf Cake, Harrison Cake, Bread Cake, Yellow Cake, Snow Cake, Silver Cake, Gold Cake, Pound Cake, Welcome Cake, Indiana Cake, Daisy Cake, Angel Cake, Rock Cake, Coffee Cake, Dover Cake, French Cake, Plain Cake, Buckeye Cake, Beautiful Cake, White Mountain Cake, Measure Cake, Dried Apple Fruit Cake, Feather Cake, Shetburn Cake, Queen Cake, Marble Cake, Tennessee Cake, Graham Cake, Saffron Cake, Black Cake, Jackson Cake, Cheap Fruit Cake, Delicate Cake, Jelly-Roll Cake, Cheap and Good Sponge Cake, Ginger Bread, Ginger Cake, Japanese Cake, Cocoanut Cake, Cream Rose Cake, Neapolitan Cake, Almond Cream Cake, Orange Cake, Josephus Cake, Jelly Cake, Velvet Sponge Cake, Delicious Cake, Ginger Cup Cake, Apple Lemon Cake, Lemon Jelly Cake, Corn-Starch Custard Cake, Rocky Mountain Cake, Mount Blanc Cake, Tea Cakes, Ginger Cakes, Ginger Snaps, Hoffman's Doughnuts, Almond Doughnuts, Sand Tarts, Raised Doughnuts, Baking-Powder Doughnuts, Cream Cookies, Cream Cullers, Ice Cream Cake, Raisin Cake, Orange Cake, Bride's Cake, Watermelon Cake, Wedding Cake, Madison Cake, Order of Mixing Cake.................90–133

Additional Cake Recipes............................181–183

SAUCES.

Pickle Sauce, Vegetable Sauce, Mushroom Sauce, Lemon Sauce, Liquid Pudding Sauce, Plain Pudding Sauce, Hard Pudding Sauce, Brown Sauce, Drawn Butter Sauce.......134–135

PAGE.
CUSTARDS AND CREAMS.

Meringue Custard, Chocolate Custard, Frozen Custard, Ice Cream, Chocolate Ice Cream, Fruit Ice Cream, Strawberry Ice Cream, Raspberry Ice Cream, Banana Ice Cream, Lemon Ice, Strawberry Ice, Orange Ice, Currant Ice, Frozen Strawberries, Lemon Float.................................136–139

DRINKS.

Coffee, Strained Coffee, Boiled Coffee, Milk Coffee, Cold-Water Coffee, Tea, Chocolate, Children's Tea, Cold Lemonade, Hot Lemonade, Warm Milk, Invalid's Drink, Gruel, Beef Tea, Infant's Food..............................141–144

CANNING FRUIT.

Time for Boiling, and Quantity of Sugar in one Quart Fruit.....145

PRESERVES.

Watermelon Preserves, Citron Preserves, Spiced Grapes, Grape Butter, Crystal Jelly, Grape Jelly, Sweet Pickles, Virginia Sweet Pickles, Watermelon Sweet Pickles, Peach Pickle, Baked Apples, Stewed Apples, Sweet-Pickled Cucumbers, Pieplant, Stewed Figs, Cranberry Jelly, Currant Jelly, Plum Jelly, Grape Jelly, Apple Jelly, Gelatine Jelly, Grape Jam, Blackberry Jam, Raspberry Jam, Quince Jam..................146–151

CANDY.

Boston Caramels, Chocolate Caramels, Cocoanut Caramels, Caramel Cake, Cocoanut Candy, Sugar Candy, Fig Candy, Butterscotch, Cocoanut Puffs, Hickorynut Candy, Chocolate Candy, Nut Candy, Taffy...................................152–155

MISCELLANEOUS.

Miscellaneous 155–171

ADDITIONAL RECIPES.

Calf-Head Soup, Beef Soup, Clear Vegetable Soup, Milk Soup, For Curing Meat, To Make Steak Tender, Veal Loaf, Washington Chow-Chow, Mangoes, Sweet Pickles, Chinese Pickles, Curry Powder, New England Brown Bread, Graham and Indian Brown Bread, Floating Island, Suet Pudding, Currant Pudding, Steamed Fruit Pudding, Scotch Pie, Orange Pie, Vinegar Pie, Mock Mince Pie, Apple Pie, Cream Pie, Apple Meringue, Transparent Pie, Italian Cream, Lemon Sponge, Lemon Butter, Preserved Oranges, Guava Jelly, Preserved Citron, Orange or Lemon Marmalade, Ginger Crackers, Hickorynut Macaroni, Drop Cake, Baker's Pound Cake, Tea Cake, Dolly Varden Cake, To Ice a Cake, Date Cake, Citron Cake, Marble Cake, Ambrosia Cake, Imperial Cake 172–183

INDEX TO ADDITIONAL RECIPES.

Soups 172–173
Meats 173–174
Pickles, etc 174–176
Bread 175
Puddings 175–177
Pies 177–179
Preserves 180
Cakes 181–183

KITCHEN UTENSILS.

Kitchen Utensils 183–184

www.ingramcontent.com/pod-product-compliance
Lightning Source LLC
Chambersburg PA
CBHW021350230426
43666CB00006B/471